MASTERING NEW YORK'S INTERMEDIATE SOCIAL STUDIES STANDARDS

JAMES KILLORAN

STUART ZIMMER

MARK JARRETT

JARRETT PUBLISHING COMPANY

EAST COAST OFFICE
P.O. Box 1460
Ronkonkoma, NY 11779
631-981-4248

WEST COAST OFFICE
10 Folin Lane
Lafayette, CA 94549
925-906-9742

1-800-859-7679 ❖ Fax: 631-588-4722
www.jarrettpub.com

About Our Cover: On April 16, 1789, two days after receiving notification of his election, George Washington left his home in Virginia for New York City. On inauguration day, the city was crowded with people. At half past noon, Washington rode alone from his quarters to the corner of Wall and Nassau Streets. Arriving at Federal Hall, Washington walked onto the balcony. Robert Livingston, Chancellor of New York, administered the oath of office. After taking the oath, thirteen cannons — one for each state — were fired, concluding the young nation's first inaugural ceremony.

The authors want to thank the following educators who reviewed the manuscript. Their comments, suggestions, and recommendations proved invaluable.

Barbara Bernard, teacher
Past President, New York State
Council for Social Studies
William T. Rogers Middle School
Kings Park, New York

Elizabeth F. Guardenier, teacher
Department Chairperson
Fox Lane Middle School
Bedford, New York

Robert Dytell, teacher
Social Studies Congruence Specialist
Alternative School Superintendency
Long Island City, New York

Sue Owens, teacher
K–12 Social Studies Department, Chairperson
Columbia High School
East Greenbush, New York

Maps and graphics by C.F. Enterprises, Huntington, New York.

Layout, graphics and typesetting: Burmar Technical Corporation, Albertson, NY.

This book is dedicated…

to Donna, Christian, Carrie, and Jesse,
and my grandchildren Aiden and Christian

— James Killoran

to Joan, Todd, and Ronald,
and my grandchildren Jared and Katie

— Stuart Zimmer

to Gośka, Alexander, and Julia

— Mark Jarrett

ISBN 1-882422-87-2

Printed in the United States of America

First Edition

10 9 8 7 6 5 4 3   07 06

ABOUT THE AUTHORS

James Killoran is a retired Assistant Principal. He has written *Government and You* and *Economics and You*. Mr. Killoran has extensive experience in test writing for the N.Y. State Board of Regents in Social Studies and has served on the Committee for Testing of the N.C.S.S. His article on social studies testing has been published in *Social Education,* the country's leading social studies journal. In addition, Mr. Killoran has won a number of awards for outstanding teaching and curriculum development, including "Outstanding Social Studies Teacher" and "Outstanding Social Studies Supervisor" in New York City. In 1993, he was awarded an Advanced Certificate for Teachers of Social Studies by the N.C.S.S. In 1997, he became Chairman of the N.C.S.S. Committee on Awarding Advanced Certificates for Teachers of Social Studies.

Stuart Zimmer is a retired Social Studies teacher. He has written *Government and You* and *Economics and You*. He served as a test writer for the N.Y. State Board of Regents in Social Studies, and has written for the National Merit Scholarship Examination. In addition Mr. Zimmer has published numerous articles on teaching and testing in Social Studies journals. He has presented many educational workshops at local, state, and national teachers' conferences. In 1989, Mr. Zimmer's achievements were recognized by the New York State Legislature with a Special Legislative Resolution in his honor.

Mark Jarrett is a former Social Studies teacher and attorney. Mr. Jarrett has served as a test writer for the New York State Board of Regents, and has taught at Hofstra University. He was educated at Columbia University, the London School of Economics, the Law School of the University of California at Berkeley, and Stanford University, where he is a doctoral candidate in history. Mr. Jarrett has received several academic awards including the Order of the Coif at Berkeley and the David and Christina Phelps Harris Fellowship at Stanford.

ALSO BY KILLORAN, ZIMMER, AND JARRETT

Mastering New York's Grade 5 Social Studies Standards
The Key to Understanding U.S. History and Government
Mastering U.S. History
Historia y gobierno de los Estados Unidos
Mastering Ohio's 9th Grade Citizenship Test
Mastering Ohio's 12th Grade Citizenship Test
Los Estados Unidos: Su Historia, Su Gobierno
Ohio: The Buckeye State
Ohio: Its Neighbors, Near and Far
Principios de economía
Texas: Its Land and Its People
New York: Its Land and Its People
North Carolina: The Tar Heel State
Michigan: Its Land and Its People
The Key to Understanding Global History
Mastering Global History
Claves para la comprensión de historial universal
Mastering the M.E.A.P. Test in Social Studies: Grade 5
Mastering the M.E.A.P. Test in Social Studies: Grade 8

TABLE OF CONTENTS

INTRODUCTION

Throughout this school year, you will study American history and culture. **Culture** refers to the traditions, beliefs and ways of doing things that unite a people.

Americans share many common experiences and ideas that bind them together. First, they occupy the same geographic area in North America. They live on a continent richly endowed with vast natural resources and open space, and this has helped shape our culture. Secondly, Americans come from different origins. Even the most ancient Americans, the American Indians, migrated here from Asia. Because of their mixed backgrounds, Americans were able to blend many of the best features of several cultures. Americans also learned the importance of tolerating differences. At a time when people of different religions in Europe were fighting one another, several colonies in British North America introduced traditions of religious freedom and the separation of church and state. Finally, Americans embraced the ideal of democratic government, taking English and European ideas and developing them even further in the Declaration of Independence and U.S. Constitution. Individual liberty, equality before the law, and representative government are basic elements of American culture.

Sometime during this school year, you will be asked to take New York's **Grade 8 Intermediate Social Studies Test**. This book will help you to succeed on this important test. Let's start your preparation by learning more about this test. There will be three type of questions on the test.

MULTIPLE-CHOICE QUESTIONS

There will be 45 **multiple-choice questions,** each with four possible choices. Your task will be to select the best choice from among the four choices.

CONSTRUCTED-RESPONSE QUESTIONS

There will be three or four **constructed-response questions** on the test. A constructed-response question is an open-ended question based on examining a piece of data such as a timeline, map, graph, cartoon, or chart. Your answer should be brief, consisting of only a few words or sentences.

DOCUMENT-BASED ESSAY QUESTION

There will be one **document-based essay question.** This question will test your ability to interpret and draw conclusions from historical documents. The document-based question will be made up of two parts:

★ Questions about each document asking for short written responses similar to constructed-response questions — called *scaffolding*.

★ An essay question that requires you to use information from the documents, and your knowledge of social studies in your answer.

ANALYSIS OF THE EIGHTH GRADE TEST

The following chart indicates the number of items, the time permitted for each type, and the weight given to each part of the test.

Type of Question	Number of Items	Time	Weight
Multiple-Choice	45	40 minutes	50%
Constructed-Response	3 to 4	30 minutes	20%
Document-Based Essay	1	90 minutes	30% • 10% short responses (*scaffolding*) • 20% essay

By paying careful attention to your teachers at school, by completing your homework assignments, and by preparing with this book, you can be confident that you will do your best when the day of the test arrives.

CHAPTER 1

THE BASIC TOOLS OF SOCIAL STUDIES

WHAT IS HISTORY?

History is the story of the past. People who study and write about history are known as **historians.** Historians are concerned with understanding events that happened in the past and with learning about the ideas, actions, and beliefs of people who lived in the past. Historians study history because it helps society to identify who we are, where we've been, and where we're going. Just as your own life would be meaningless if you had no memory of who you were or what you had done, each society looks to its history for a sense of its own identity. Just as we remember those in the past, we hope future generations will recall what we have done.

SOURCES OF HISTORY

In one sense, a historian is much like a detective. Both detectives and historians work at gathering clues. To find information about the past, historians rely on two kinds of sources:

★ **Primary Sources** are the original records of an event. They include documents left by eyewitnesses, records created at the time of the event, speeches, diaries, reports, letters by people involved in the event, photographs, and artifacts. Interviews of eyewitnesses who were alive at the time of the event are also primary sources. All historical knowledge can eventually be traced back to primary sources.

★ **Secondary Sources** are the later writings and interpretations of historians and other writers. Often secondary sources, like textbooks and articles, provide convenient summaries and analyses of the information found in primary sources.

DEVELOPING A SENSE OF TIME AND PLACE

It is important to have a good grasp of **time** and **place** when studying history. American history covers the time from the arrival of Native American Indians on this continent to the present. In order to understand this vast sweep of time, you must:

★ **First,** have a strong general sense of the basic time periods of American history, including the major events, people, beliefs and ideas of each period;

★ **Second,** know the main geographical features of the United States — the stage where these historical developments unfolded.

DEVELOPING A SENSE OF TIME

Historians divide history into **time periods** — time spans unified by common characteristics — making the past easier to understand. There is no exact agreement on historical periods and their dates. Different periods may begin and end in different places at different times. How history is divided depends on what a historian thinks is important. Many historical periods have traditionally been tied to a particular event. For example, the American Revolutionary period is closely tied to the struggle of the American colonies for independence between 1775 and 1783. This book divides American history into six major periods, each with its own features and major characteristics:

★ The Road to Independence, from Earliest Times to 1783

★ The New Nation: Birth and Growth, from 1783 to 1840

★ The Union Tested, from 1840 to 1877

★ The Industrialization of America, from 1877 to 1918

★ From Progressivism to the New Deal, from 1898 to 1941

★ The United States as a World Leader, from 1941 to the Present

DEVELOPING A SENSE OF PLACE: PHYSICAL REGIONS OF THE UNITED STATES

A **region** is an area that shares certain common features. Places within a region have greater contact with other places within the region than with the outside. Because of its diverse topography and climate, the continental United States can be thought of as consisting of several geographic regions. In fact, there are many ways to divide the United States into regions. One way of doing so is as follows:

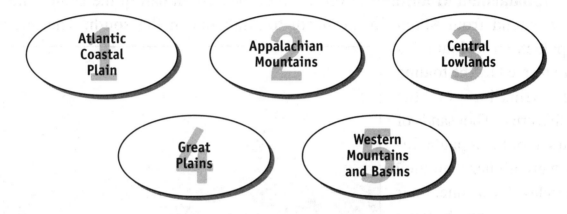

1. Atlantic Coastal Plain
2. Appalachian Mountains
3. Central Lowlands
4. Great Plains
5. Western Mountains and Basins

The locations of these five regions are indicated on the map below:

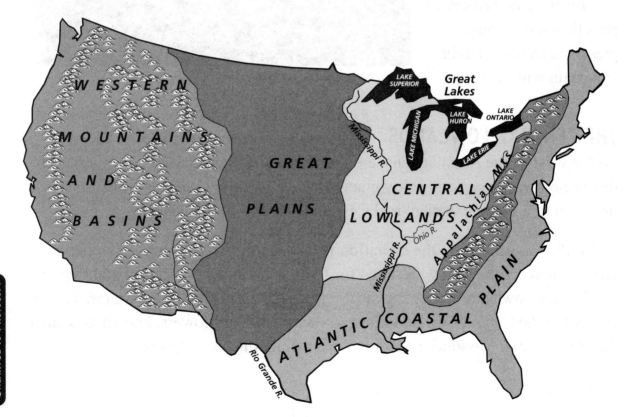

THE ATLANTIC COASTAL PLAIN

The **Atlantic Coastal Plain** stretches southward from New England to Georgia. From Georgia it widens out to Texas while continuing southward. Much of this area was forest before settlers turned it into farmland. The Atlantic Coastal Plain rises up to a hilly area, known as the **Piedmont,** as it approaches the Appalachians.

THE APPALACHIAN MOUNTAINS

The **Appalachian Mountains** cover much of the eastern part of the United States. They extend from Maine in the north to Alabama in the south. The ancient

Appalachian Mountains were formed by the folding and wrinkling of the Earth's crust. Thousands of years ago, the Appalachians were higher than they are today. Over time, their peaks eroded and became rounded. They were difficult for the first settlers to pass through because they presented an almost unbroken chain with few gaps.

N.C. Travel and Tourism

The Great Smoky Mountains in Western North Carolina

THE CENTRAL LOWLANDS

To the west of the Appalachians are the **Central Lowlands.** The northern part of this region was once scraped by glaciers (*huge moving sheets of ice*) and is a continuation of a sheet of ancient rocks extending down from Canada.

Farther south, where the elevation is lower, glaciers and winds deposited soil and silt, making the land well suited for farming. Windblown topsoil makes parts of the Central Lowlands among the most fertile regions of the United States. The eastern part of the Central Lowlands are grasslands and wildflowers, known as **prairies.** The Mississippi, Missouri, and Ohio Rivers drain this vast region.

THE GREAT PLAINS

West of the Mississippi, the grasslands become much drier and more hilly. This region is known as the **Great Plains.** These plains were once covered with sod and grasses. Today, the Central Lowlands and the Great Plains are some of the most productive farmland in the world, providing vast amounts of corn and wheat, and large numbers of cattle, hogs, and other livestock.

Early settlers often used the rich sod of the plains to provide roofing material for their homes

Library of Congress

THE WESTERN MOUNTAINS AND BASINS

To the west of the Great Plains, the land rises sharply, forming the **Rocky Mountains.** These mountains extend from Canada as far south as New Mexico. Further west are the **Cascade** and **Sierra Nevada Ranges,** and the **Pacific Coastal Ranges.** Some of these mountains were formed by volcanoes. Most of them, like the Appalachian Mountains, were formed by the shifts and folds of the Earth's crust. Much of this region receives little rainfall.

The **Great Basin,** separating the Rocky Mountains and the Sierra Nevada, is dry and desert-like. California's Central Valley, located between the Sierra Nevada and the Coastal Range, has excellent soils, almost continuous sunshine, and a long growing season.

Much of the region west of the Great Plains consists of mountainous areas

Jarrett Archives

REMEMBERING IMPORTANT INFORMATION

Questions on the **Grade 8 Intermediate Social Studies Test** will test your knowledge of important terms, concepts and people in U.S. history. How can you be expected to remember so many important terms, concepts, and people? This section looks at one way to make it easier for you to remember important information so you can improve your performance not only on this test, but on all of your tests.

TERMS

Terms refer to specific things that actually happened or existed, such as particular places or events. Questions about a term usually ask about its main features:

1. what it is (or was)
2. its purpose
3. its causes and effects
4. its significance

CONCEPTS

Concepts are words or phrases that refer to categories of information, allowing us to organize large amounts of information. For example, the American Revolution, Civil War, World War I, and Korean Conflict share common characteristics. The concept *war* acts as an umbrella, grouping these specific "examples" by identifying what they have in common. Questions about concepts usually ask for a definition or an example. Thus, when you study a concept, you should learn the following:

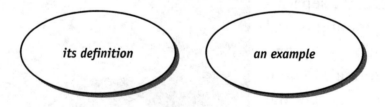

its definition   an example

FAMOUS PEOPLE

In U.S. history you will also learn about many famous people. Test questions about these individuals will usually ask you who they are and why they are famous.

Therefore, when you study a famous person, it is important to learn:

the place and time period in which the person lived **1**

his or her background or position **2**

the person's accomplishments and impact **3**

To help you remember important terms, concepts, and people, you should complete index cards. Let's look at what information each card should contain:

★ **Front of the Card:** Write out the important information.

★ **Back of the Card:** An illustration about the item.

Look at the example below that has been completed for a term:

Note: Turning written information into an illustration helps you to clarify the meaning of the term. The ability to change a term from one medium (*words*) into another medium (*an illustration*) is only possible if you truly understand the term or concept. By "seeing" the key points of a term or concept, you create an impression in your mind that will help you to remember the term.

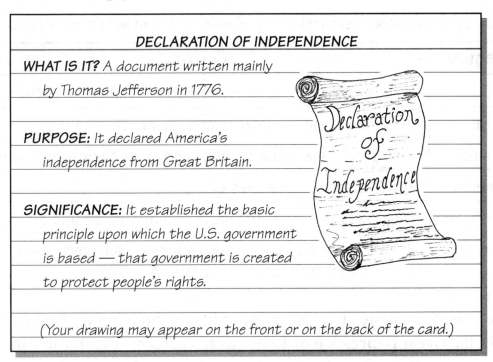

DECLARATION OF INDEPENDENCE

WHAT IS IT? A document written mainly by Thomas Jefferson in 1776.

PURPOSE: It declared America's independence from Great Britain.

SIGNIFICANCE: It established the basic principle upon which the U.S. government is based — that government is created to protect people's rights.

(Your drawing may appear on the front or on the back of the card.)

Here is what a sample card would look like that has been completed for a concept:

```
┌─────────────────────────────────────────────────────────────────┐
│                           DEMOCRACY                               │
│                                                                   │
│   DEFINITION: A system of government                              │
│      in which people govern themselves,                           │
│      usually through elected representatives.    BALLOT           │
│                                                                   │
│   EXAMPLE: The system of government           BALLOT              │
│      found in the United States is a           BOX               │
│      representative democracy.                                    │
│                                                                   │
│      (Your drawing may appear on the front or back of the card.)  │
└─────────────────────────────────────────────────────────────────┘
```

To help you identify the most important terms, concepts, and people, these will be highlighted in **bold** print throughout the content chapters of this book. We suggest that you create a set of index cards when you complete each content chapter. By the time of the test, you will have a collection of cards to help you review.

CLASSIFYING INFORMATION

Another way to remember information is to **classify** it into major themes of social studies:

Category	Content
Social	How people relate in groups, such as families or social classes
Political	How people choose leaders and govern themselves
Economic	How people make their livings and meet their everyday needs
Geographic	The location and features of a place
Cultural	People's beliefs and customs, including music and art
Religious	Beliefs about God and organizations of believers, such as churches, synagogues or mosques

When you learn more about an event, or idea or practice, try to classify it. For example, the **Great Depression of 1929** was an economic event, while the **Harlem Renaissance** would be considered a cultural event.

CHAPTER 2

INTERPRETING DIFFERENT TYPES OF DATA

On the **Grade 8 Intermediate Social Studies Test,** questions will often ask you to apply what you know to interpreting a piece of data. You cannot answer such questions until you *understand the data* presented in the question. In this chapter, you will examine the major types of data that may appear on the test:

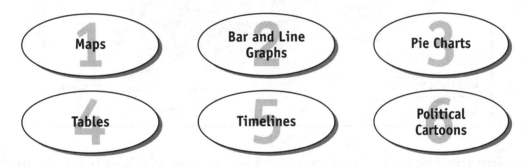

1. Maps
2. Bar and Line Graphs
3. Pie Charts
4. Tables
5. Timelines
6. Political Cartoons

MAPS

A **map** is a drawing of a geographic area. There are many kinds of maps:

★ **Political maps** show the major boundaries between countries or states.

★ **Physical maps** show physical characteristics of a region, such as rivers, mountains, vegetation, and elevation (*height above sea level*).

★ **Product maps** provide information on the major natural resources and agricultural and industrial products of an area.

★ **Theme maps** provide information on the theme of the map, such as rainfall, languages spoken, temperatures, or main points of interest.

★ **Globes** are three-dimensional "maps" representing the entire world.

STEPS TO UNDERSTANDING A MAP

1. **Look at the Title.** The map title tells you what kind of information is presented. For example, the title of the map below indicates that this map is about the Union and Confederate states during the Civil War.

2. **Examine the Legend.** The legend, or **key,** lists the symbols used and identifies what they represent. In this map:

   the horizontal lines show "free" (*non-slave*) states that remained loyal to the Union during the Civil War

   the diagonal lines show which "border" (*slave*) states remained loyal to the Union

   the light gray areas show which states seceded (*withdrew*) from the Union and formed the Confederate States of America

3. **Check the Compass Rose.** The compass rose shows the four basic directions — north, south, east, and west. If there is no compass rose, assume north is at the top and south is at the bottom of the map.

4. **View the Scale.** A map would be impossible to use if it were the same size as the area it shows. Mapmakers reduce the size so that it can fit onto a page. A scale is used to indicate the real distance between places on a map.

Map scales are often shown as a line marked "**Scale of Miles.**" Scales usually provide the distance in miles or kilometers. For example, one inch may be equal to one mile. Or the mapmaker may use one inch to represent 100 miles.

FINDING SPECIFIC INFORMATION

To find specific information, you often have to use the legend and other map features. For example, if you wanted to find how many states seceded during the Civil War, here is what you must do:

★ Carefully examine the legend to determine which states withdrew from the Union and became members of the Confederate States of America. The legend shows that the states shaded gray seceded from the Union.

★ Locate the states on the map that are shaded gray. Count the number of states shaded gray. Thus, there were eleven states that seceded during the Civil War.

✔ CHECKING YOUR UNDERSTANDING ✔

1. Name two Western states on the map on page 12 that remained loyal to the Union.
2. Was New York State a free, border, or Confederate state during the Civil War?

BAR AND LINE GRAPHS

There are many types of graphs. A **bar graph** is made up of parallel bars with different lengths. It is used to show a comparison of two or more things. Another type graph is a **line graph.** It is composed of a series of points connected by a line. Line graphs are often used to show how something has changed over a period of time.

STEPS TO UNDERSTANDING GRAPHS

1. Look at the Title. The graph's title tells you what information is being presented. For example, the title of the bar graph on the next page tells you from which regions of the world immigrants came to the United States between 1900 and 1995.

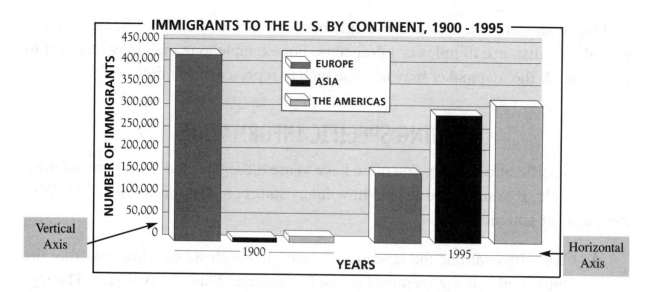

2. **Examine the Key.** It identifies what each bar or point on a line graph represents. In the graph above:

★ the dark gray bars represent Europe

★ the black bars represent Asia

★ the light gray bars represent the Americas (*North and South America*)

3. **Look at the Vertical and Horizontal Axes.**

★ The **vertical axis** runs from top to bottom on the left-hand side of the graph. It usually measures the length of the bars or the height of a line graph. In the bar graph above, the *number of immigrants* — from 0 to 450,000 — is listed in the vertical axis in thousands.

★ The **horizontal axis** runs from left to right. It usually identifies the bars or the points on a line graph. Here, the horizontal axis indicates the *years* being compared: 1900 and 1995.

FINDING SPECIFIC INFORMATION

To find specific information on a bar or line graph, you must closely examine the features of the graph. For example, to find out how many immigrants came to the United States from Europe in 1900, here is what you must do:

★ On the horizontal axis, locate the year *1900*.

★ Choose the bar that represents *Europe*. According to the legend, this is the dark gray bar.

★ Run your finger to the top of the bar, and slide it slightly to the left. When you reach the vertical axis, you will find it is between *400,000* and *450,000*. This shows the number of immigrants from Europe in 1900 was about 425,000.

✔ CHECKING YOUR UNDERSTANDING ✔

1. Using the bar graph appearing on page 14, in which year shown — 1900 or 1995 — did the *least* number of people come from Europe to the United States?

2. About how many immigrants came to the United States from Asia in 1995?

PIE CHARTS

A **pie chart,** also called a **circle graph,** is a circle divided into sections of different sizes. It is used to show relationships between a whole and its parts.

STEPS TO UNDERSTANDING A PIE CHART

1. **Look at the Title.** The title identifies the overall topic. For example, this pie chart shows the national origins of New Yorkers in 1990. National origin is where a person's family originally came from before arriving in the United States.

2. **Check the Slices of the Pie.** Each slice shows the size of that item in relation to the whole pie. Think of the pie as 100% of something. If you add all the slices together, they will total 100%. In this pie, six major groups made up the national origins of most New Yorkers in 1990. These groups are named on the pie slices.

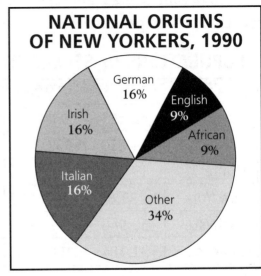

NATIONAL ORIGINS OF NEW YORKERS, 1990

German 16%
English 9%
Irish 16%
African 9%
Italian 16%
Other 34%

3. **Examine the Key.** Sometimes a pie chart has a legend showing what each slice represents. In many pie charts, a legend is not needed. Instead, the information is simply shown on the slices, as on the pie chart on page 15.

FINDING SPECIFIC INFORMATION

To find specific information, you have to examine each slice. For example, if you wanted to find out what percentage of New Yorkers trace their ancestry back to Italy, here is what you must do:

★ Begin by examining the entire pie chart carefully.

★ Locate the piece that is marked *Italian*. You can see that it represents 16% (about *one-sixth*) of the total.

✔ CHECKING YOUR UNDERSTANDING ✔

1. Using the pie chart appearing on page 15, what percentage of New Yorkers can trace their ancestry to Africa?
2. From which continent did most New Yorkers in 1990 trace their ancestry? Explain your answer.

TABLES

A **table** is an arrangement of words or numbers in columns and rows. A table is often used to organize large amounts of information so that individual facts can be easily located and compared.

POPULATIONS OF SELECT CITIES IN NEW YORK STATE, 1865–1990

City	1865	1900	1920	1940	1960	1990
Albany	62,613	94,151	113,344	130,577	129,726	100,031
Buffalo	94,210	352,387	506,775	575,901	532,759	328,175
Elmira	13,130	35,672	45,393	45,106	46,517	33,724
New York	1,123,682	3,347,202	5,620,048	7,454,995	7,781,984	7,333,253
Rochester	50,940	162,608	295,750	324,975	318,611	230,356
Syracuse	31,784	108,374	171,717	209326,	216,038	163,860

STEPS TO UNDERSTANDING A TABLE

1. **Look at the Title.** The title of the table states its topic. For example, the title indicates that the table provides information about the population of cities in New York State during selected years.

2. **Examine the Categories.** Each table has various categories of information. These categories are named in the column headings across the top of the table. In this table, there are seven different categories: *city, 1865, 1900, 1920, 1940, 1960,* and *1990.* The columns contain information for each category.

FINDING SPECIFIC INFORMATION

For specific information, you must find where the columns and rows intersect. For example, if you wanted to find Elmira's population in 1920, here is what to do:

★ Put your right index finger on the column marked *1920*. This column shows the year you are interested in finding information about.

★ Next, put your left index finger on the column marked *City*. Slide your finger down until it reaches the row for *Elmira*.

★ Finally, slide your left index finger along the *"Elmira"* row until it is in the same column as your right index finger. You can see that the total population of Elmira in 1920 was **45,393.**

✔ CHECKING YOUR UNDERSTANDING ✔

1. Using the table appearing on page 16, what was the size of New York City's population in 1960?
2. What was the largest city in New York State in 1865?
3. Identify and explain the population trends of Albany, Buffalo, and Rochester, since the 1940s.

TIMELINES

A **timeline** shows a group of events arranged in chronological order along a line. **Chronological order** is the order in which these events occurred. The first event to occur is the first event that appears on the timeline.

A timeline can span any length of time — from a short period to several thousand years. The purpose of a timeline is to show how events are related to each other. Timelines can appear horizontally or vertically. You may see them either way on the **Grade 8 Intermediate Social Studies Test.**

KEY EVENTS IN AMERICAN HISTORY

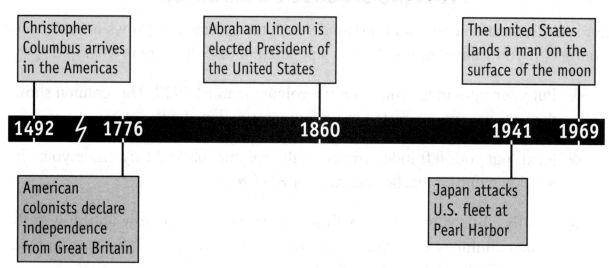

STEPS TO UNDERSTANDING A TIMELINE

1. **Look at the Title.** The title tells you the topic or theme of the timeline. In this example, the title indicates that the timeline lists important events or "milestones" in American history.

2. **Examine the Events.** Timeline events are related in some way to the title. In this timeline, each event was a key development in American history.

3. **Be Mindful of the Dates.** Remember that events are placed on the timeline in chronological order. A timeline is always based on a particular time period, no matter how brief or long. For example, this timeline starts at the end of the 15th century (1492) and continues into the 20th century (1969).

If you add a new event, the date might fall between two dates on the timeline. For example, if you wanted to add the start of the War of 1812, where on the timeline would you place it? Since 1812 is closer to 1776 (*36 years*) than it is to 1860 (*48 years*), you would place it on the timeline between 1776 and 1860, somewhat closer to 1776.

4. **Understand the Meanings of Special Terms.** To understand questions about timelines or time periods, you should be familiar with some special terms.

   ★ A *decade* is a ten year period.

   ★ A *century* represents a 100 year period.

   ★ A *millennium* spans a period of 1,000 years.

A Note about Identifying Centuries. Identifying centuries is often confusing. For example, the 20th century refers to the 100 years from 1901 to 2000. This numbering system came about because Western societies start counting from the time it is believed Jesus Christ was born. Thus, the first one hundred years were the years 1–100. This is called the **first century.** The second century went from 101–200; the third century was from 201 to 300, and so on. The 21st century will actually begin on January 1, 2001. However, most people celebrated it on January 1, 2000, because of the dramatic change in dates from 1999 to 2000.

---

5. **Measuring the Passage of Time.** Remember, events are arranged from the earliest event (*on the left*) to the most recent event (*on the right*). To measure the number of years from one date to another, subtract the smaller from the larger date. If it is the year 2000, how long has it been since the American colonists declared independence from Great Britain in 1776? By subtracting 1776 from 2000, we arrive at 224 years ago.

> **2000** (*assume this is the current year*)
> **– 1776** (*American colonists declare independence*)
> **224 years ago**

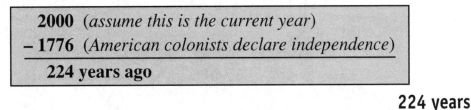

224 years

Birth of Jesus Christ

1776   2000

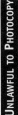

✔ CHECKING YOUR UNDERSTANDING ✔

1. Using the timeline on page 18, which event happened first: Christopher Columbus arrived in the Americas or the American colonists declared their independence from Great Britain?
2. Between which two events on the timeline would you place the completion of the transcontinental railroad in 1869?

POLITICAL CARTOONS

A **political cartoon** is a drawing that expresses an opinion about a topic or issue. Although many political cartoons are humorous, the point they make is often serious.

KEYS TO UNDERSTANDING A POLITICAL CARTOON

1. **Look at the Title or Caption.** Many political cartoons will have a title or caption. The title or caption may give some explanation of the message the cartoonist is trying to get across.

"Rough Sailing Ahead?"

2. **Look at the Parts of the Cartoon.** Cartoonists want to persuade readers to their viewpoint. To achieve this, the cartoonist will use the size of objects, expressions, exaggerations, or words spoken by its characters to make fun of some positions and to support others. Sometimes a cartoonist simply wants to draw attention to a particular issue.

3. **Be Aware of Symbols.** Cartoonists often use symbols. A **symbol** can be any object that stands for, or *represents,* something else. For example, an elephant sometimes represents the Republican Party, while a donkey represents the Democratic Party.

INTERPRETING A POLITICAL CARTOON

To understand a cartoon, it helps to know something about the situation it illustrates. Examine the cartoon on the opposite page, then review the background to the situation the cartoonist has chosen to illustrate:

After declaring independence from Great Britain in 1776, each of the thirteen colonies became an independent state. The states soon realized the need for some type of national (*central*) government. In 1781, the states adopted the **Articles of Confederation.** The central government created by the Articles of Confederation was weak. It lacked many important powers, such as the power to collect taxes or raise an army. Many people believed the central government under the Articles was too weak to survive.

FINDING SPECIFIC INFORMATION

To understand the cartoon, you must examine the drawing carefully.

★ The cartoonist has drawn a large sailing ship. The ship represents or symbolizes the central government under the Articles of Confederation. It is sailing through very rough waters. Notice how the waves reach high up onto the ship, almost threatening to sink it.

★ The waves are a key feature of the cartoon. Each wave symbolizes a different weakness facing the central government under the Articles of Confederation — no national court system, no power to enforce treaties or laws, and no power to raise an army.

★ The caption states, "Rough Sailing Ahead?" With such a caption, the cartoonist seems to be questioning whether the central government under the Articles of Confederation is in danger of sinking.

✔ CHECKING YOUR UNDERSTANDING ✔

1. Describe the situation shown in the cartoon on page 20.
2. Which items has the cartoonist exaggerated or highlighted?
3. What do you think is the main idea of the cartoon?

INTERPRETING DOCUMENTS

A **document** usually consists of written material about a particular topic or subject. You might be asked a question about a document that is simply a quotation or a short paragraph. You will learn how to interpret documents in a later chapter.

THE HISTORICAL METHOD REVISITED

Now that you know more about different types of data, let's look again at the work done by historians. Historians investigate important events and developments by asking questions, such as:

★ What were the causes of this event?

★ How were these different developments related?

Like scientists, historians often begin with a "hunch" or hypothesis to answer the question. Then they research their hypothesis by looking at primary and secondary sources, including historical documents, maps, graphs, cartoons and tables. Historians try to gather as many facts as they can about the issue they are investigating. They also recognize opinions and different points of view. They discard what is **irrelevant** — unimportant or not meaningful — and select only information that is **relevant** to the question they are exploring. Then they see if their beginning hypothesis was correct based on the facts they have gathered. Finally, they draw meaningful conclusions about the event or development under study.

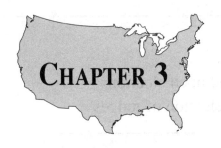

CHAPTER 3

HOW TO ANSWER MULTIPLE-CHOICE QUESTIONS

This chapter focuses on answering multiple-choice questions. The 45 multiple-choice questions on the test can be grouped into:

> ★ **Statement Questions.** These types of questions begin with a question or an incomplete statement followed by a list of four choices or ways in which the statement can be completed.
>
> ★ **Data-based Questions.** These types of questions present a piece of data or information as part of the question. You are then asked some question about the data, to which you respond by selecting the correct answer from a list of four choices.

Multiple-choice questions test how well you have mastered basic social studies skills and content. Testmakers do this with a variety of question styles.

DEMONSTRATING KNOWLEDGE OF IMPORTANT INFORMATION

Multiple-choice questions often test your knowledge of important terms, concepts, and people. The following is an example of how these questions may be phrased:

1. The concept of *democracy* is best illustrated by

    1 a single political party   3 free and open elections

    2 equal rights for minorities   4 direct election of judges

> *The best answer is **3**. Democracies can have one political party, equal rights for minorities, and direct election of judges. However, the very definition of a democracy is government by the people. Thus, a democracy must have free and open elections.*
>
> *To help you recognize major terms, concepts, and people, these will be highlighted in **bold type** when they first appear in this book. Also, you should create your own set of index cards for the most important terms, concepts, and people listed at the end of each content chapter.*

ANALYZING DATA

Comprehension questions test whether you understand data presented as part of a data-based question. The following example illustrates one way a comprehension question may be phrased:

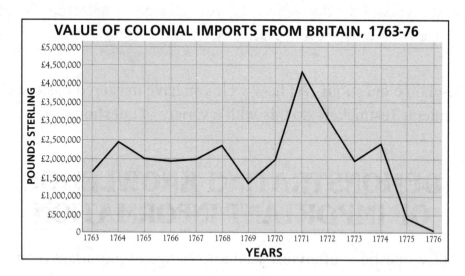

2. What was the total value of colonial imports from Britain in 1763?

    1 £1,500,000   3 £1,900,000

    2 £1,650,000   4 £2,000,000

> *The best answer is **2**. This can be seen by looking at the dates along the bottom of the graph. Start by locating the year 1763. Move up along the 1763 line. When you reach the vertical axis it shows the value of imports along the left side of the graph. These two points intersect somewhere between £1,500,000 and £2,000,000 — but closer to £1,500,000. To help you answer data-based questions, practice questions are provided throughout this book.*

UNDERSTANDING A GENERALIZATION

Some questions will test your ability to draw a conclusion or to make a generalization. A **generalization** is a general statement identifying a relationship found in several specific examples. The following example shows how this question may appear:

3. Which statement is most accurate about family life in Colonial America?

  1 All families had pets.
  2 Men and women had equal authority.
  3 Women and children were supposed to obey the father.
  4 Most couples did not have children.

> *The best answer is **3**. Men had final authority in colonial families. The other choices are incorrect. To help you answer this type of question, important generalizations are emphasized throughout this book.*

COMPARING AND CONTRASTING

Comparing and contrasting allows us to separate people, events, ideas and concepts, in order to understand them more clearly. Such a question might appear as:

4. *George Washington* and *Thomas Jefferson* were similar in that both

  1 helped write the Declaration of Independence
  2 served as Presidents during the Articles of Confederation
  3 gave the nation stability as early Presidents
  4 were generals during the American Revolution

*The correct answer is **3**. Washington did not help draft the Declaration of Independence. Jefferson was never a general. There were no Presidents under the Articles of Confederation. As you read each chapter, compare and contrast **new** terms, concepts and people with those you already know.*

IDENTIFYING CAUSE AND EFFECT

History consists of a series of events leading to other events. The explanation of why an event came about gives history much of its meaning. Cause-and-effect questions test your understanding of the relationship between an action or event, its causes, and its effects. In answering these questions, be careful to understand what is being asked for — the *cause* or the *effect*. Such questions might appear as follows:

5. **Which was a major cause of the War of 1812?**

    1 British impressment of American sailors
    2 dispute over the southern border of Texas
    3 disagreement over the extension of slavery
    4 U.S. invasion of Canada

> **asks for a *cause***

*The correct answer is **1**. The other events were not causes of the War of 1812. The southern border of Texas was a cause of the Mexican-American War. The extension of slavery was a cause of the Civil War. Although the U.S. did invade Canada during the War of 1812, it was not a cause of the war.*

6. **Which was a result of the construction of the Erie Canal?**

    1 increased trade through New York City
    2 New York State faced financial ruin
    3 Dutch patroon system collapsed
    4 elimination of cities along the canal route

> **asks for an *effect***

*The correct answer is **1**. The Erie Canal led to increased shipments down the Hudson River to New York City. The other answers are incorrect. New York did not face financial ruin, cities were not eliminated, and the Dutch patroon system ended much earlier in history. To help you answer cause-and-effect questions, major causal relationships are identified in each content chapter.*

DETERMINING CHRONOLOGY

Events listed in **chronological order** start from the earliest event and progress to the latest one. Questions about chronological order might appear as:

7. **Which group of events is in correct chronological order?**

    1 War of 1812, ratification of the Constitution, Albany Plan of Union
    2 Albany Plan of Union, Stamp Act, Mayflower Compact
    3 Stamp Act, Civil War, Boston Tea Party
    4 Mayflower Compact, Albany Plan of Union, War of 1812

*The correct answer is **4**. The other lists of events are not in chronological order. The War of 1812 occurred after the ratification of the Constitution. The Stamp Act was passed after the Mayflower Compact. The Civil War occurred after the Boston Tea Party.*

DISTINGUISHING FACT FROM OPINION

Some questions will ask you to distinguish between fact and opinion.

★ A **fact** is a statement that can be proven to be true. For example, the following is a factual statement: "Many colonists remained loyal to the British during the American Revolution." We often check the truthfulness of a factual statement by looking at several sources, especially primary sources.

★ An **opinion** is an expression of someone's belief and can't be proven true. An example would be: "Loyalists were the bravest soldiers in the British army."

Questions asking you to distinguish fact from opinion could be phrased as:

8. **Which statement about the Iroquois expresses an opinion?**

    1 The Cayuga, Mohawk, Seneca, and Oneida were Iroquois tribes.
    2 Many Iroquois people spent their winters living in longhouses.
    3 The Iroquois were the best Native American Indian warriors.
    4 Iroquois men built canoes for fishing and trading with other villages.

*The correct answer is **3**. The other statements are all facts that can be proven. However, the phrase "best Native American Indian warriors" is an opinion that cannot be proven.*

APPLYING RESEARCH SKILLS

Historians and social scientists consult a wide variety of sources in order to discover what has happened in the past. Some questions may ask you to identify a specialized book of information. One standard reference book is an **atlas,** which contains a collection of maps. Other standard reference books are **encyclopedias** and **almanacs.** An **encyclopedia** is a book or set of books containing articles on various subjects, arranged in alphabetical order. An **almanac** is a book published annually that includes useful and interesting information about countries, sports, etc.

Other types of sources historians and social scientists often use include:

★ **Periodicals:** These are newspapers, magazines, or any other publication that appears in regular time periods.

★ **Computer Databases:** Social scientists might use information stored in a computer.

★ **Census Reports:** These reports tell how many people live in a region and their characteristics. The U.S. has a national census every ten years.

★ **Interviews:** Social scientists sometimes interview people to find out their opinions or views.

★ **Internet Websites:** As more information is placed on the world-wide web, the Internet becomes an increasingly important research tool.

Questions asking you about your research skills might appear as:

9. **To find information about New York State's topography, which would be the best source to consult?**

    1 an atlas   3 an almanac
    2 a dictionary   4 an American history textbook

*The correct answer is **1**. Although each of the other sources may contain some information on New York State's topography, the best source would be an atlas. An atlas is a book designed to provide maps and topographical information.*

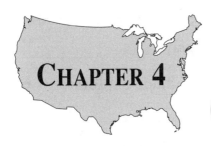

CHAPTER 4

HOW TO ANSWER CONSTRUCTED-RESPONSE QUESTIONS

Some examination questions require you to write out answers rather than choose from a list of possible answers. These questions are called **constructed-response questions.** They begin with a piece of data. It might be a map, table, political cartoon, graph, chart, timeline, or short passage. This is followed by a series of questions in which you are required to write out the answer.

A MODEL CONSTRUCTED-RESPONSE QUESTION

The test will have three or four constructed-response questions. Following is a model constructed-response question. Let's begin by examining it.

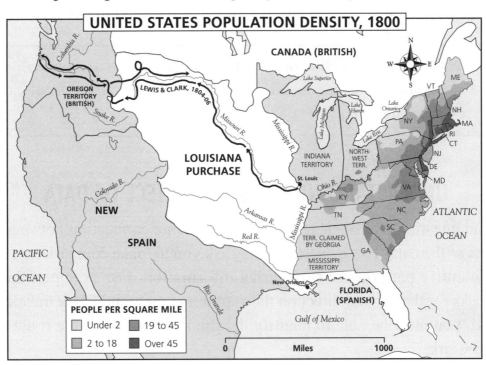

1. What was the population density of North Carolina in 1800? _____

2. In what general direction did Lewis and Clark travel in their explorations of 1804 to 1806? _____

3. Describe one effect of the Louisiana Purchase on the United States. _____

_____

Notice that the questions progress from simple comprehension questions to more difficult questions that ask you to apply or explain the data. Let's look at each type of question more closely.

UNDERSTANDING PARTS OF THE DATA

The first question will usually test your understanding of some part of the data. In each of these types of questions, you may be asked to *name* or *identify* some major feature of the data. Some key words used in this type of question are: ***name, identify, give, who, what, when,*** and ***where.*** The word ***list*** is often used when the question asks for more than one answer or piece of information.

In the first question, you are asked ***what*** the population density of North Carolina was in 1800. The answer to this question can be found in the data itself.

You can see from the shading of North Carolina (*light gray*) and by examining the legend on the map that its population density ranged from 2 to 18 persons per square mile.

UNDERSTANDING THE WHOLE PIECE OF DATA

The second question will often ask you to make some connection between the different parts of the data. These questions may ask you to make comparisons, find similarities, identify patterns, or summarize information. For example, the second question asks for the general direction the explorers Lewis and Clark traveled. Using the legend, you must be able to identify the thick black line as the route taken by Lewis and Clark.

To answer the question, you then must be able to follow that route to identify the general direction they took.

> The explorers Lewis and Clark first set out from St. Louis. They traveled northwest across the Louisiana Territory following the Missouri River. Later, they continued westward and crossed the Oregon Territory along the Columbia River. They followed this route until they reached the Pacific Ocean in the west. Therefore, the route they traveled was in a northwestern direction.

GOING BEYOND THE DATA

The third type of question usually asks you to bring in outside information related to the topic. You will often be asked:

★ to draw a conclusion from the data

★ to explain something about the data, or

★ to make a prediction from the data.

This type of question calls for more than just naming something. In this type of question, you are often asked to *state* or *give* reasons for something by writing one or more sentences.

For example, in the third question you were asked to describe one impact of the Louisiana Purchase on the United States. The answer to this question is ***not*** directly stated in the data. To answer this question, you must go beyond the data. You must use your prior knowledge about the impact of the Louisiana Purchase on the United States.

> The Louisiana Purchase removed the threat of a French or Spanish colony along the western frontier. The purchase also doubled the size of the nation, setting Americans on a course for continued westward expansion to the Pacific Coast.

Other ways you might be asked a question that requires you to go beyond the data are as follows:

★ What might happen if the trend shown in the table continues?

★ Based on the graph, what prediction can you make about the future of immigration to the United States?

★ Based on the chart, explain how nineteenth-century American education differed from our system of education today.

Let's practice what you have just learned by answering a constructed-response question.

<h1 align="center">A SAMPLE
CONSTRUCTED-RESPONSE QUESTION</h1>

Base your answers to questions 1 through 3 on the map to the right and your knowledge of Social Studies.

1 What does this symbol 🌲 represent? _____

2 In which colonies was tobacco production taking place? _____

_____

3 How did the geography of the New England colonies affect the goods that were produced there in 1750?

_____

_____

_____

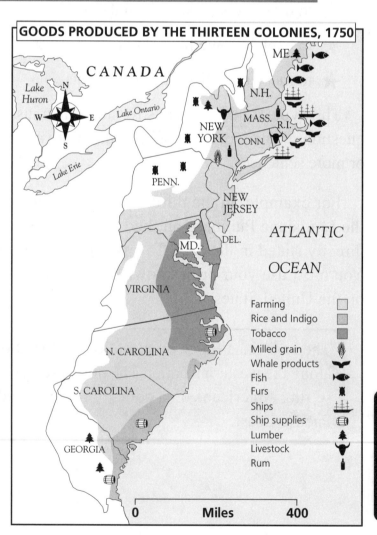

GOODS PRODUCED BY THE THIRTEEN COLONIES, 1750

Legend:
Farming
Rice and Indigo
Tobacco
Milled grain
Whale products
Fish
Furs
Ships
Ship supplies
Lumber
Livestock
Rum

0   Miles   400

THE ROAD TO INDEPENDENCE,
From Earliest Times to 1783

In this chapter, you will learn about the Native American Indians and the colonial heritage of the United States. Lastly, you will read how the American colonists fought a war against Great Britain to become an independent nation. As you read this chapter, you will learn about:

American colonists fought the British soldiers at Lexington and Concord, beginning the American Revolution

Library of Congress

★ **The First Americans.** The first people to live in the Americas came from Asia across the land bridge that once joined Alaska and Asia.

★ **Europeans Explore the Americas.** In the early 1500s, Europeans began arriving in the Americas. They soon established colonies along the Atlantic coast. As different groups arrived, a variety of lifestyles developed in different regions of the English colonies.

★ **The Road to Independence.** American colonists objected to British attempts to impose new taxes without their consent, setting off a war that led to their independence from Great Britain.

In studying this period, you should focus on the following questions:

★ What motivated Europeans to establish colonial empires in the Americas?

★ What factors led to the start of the American Revolutionary War?

★ What were the basic ideas of the Declaration of Independence?

UNLAWFUL TO PHOTOCOPY

MAJOR THEMES IN U.S. HISTORY: GEOGRAPHY

In each content chapter, following the opening section you will examine a major theme of American history. These sections are provided to deepen your understanding of major themes that run through more than one chapter.

THE FIVE THEMES OF GEOGRAPHY

Geographers have identified five major themes in the study of geography.

LOCATION

Geographers begin by considering the **location** of a place. The importance of a location may change over time. Native American Indians, for example, benefited and suffered from a location that separated them from other civilizations. For centuries, Native American Indians were protected from other continents, but they were also isolated from changes taking place in Asia, Europe, and Africa.

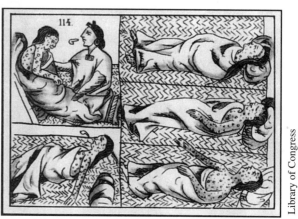

Native American Indians died from European diseases from which they had no immunity

Because of improvements in transportation, the Native American Indian empires of the Americas came within the reach of European explorers and settlers by 1492. Europe's greater population, its superior technology, and a host of new diseases like measles and smallpox had a devastating impact on the Native American Indians.

PLACE

The characteristics of a **place** — its topography, natural resources, and climate — are also important to geographers. In North America, Europeans found a continent of great beauty and natural resources. These resources turned the Americas into a magnet for European colonization.

REGION

Region refers to a geographical area that shares common characteristics. By the early 1700s, three distinct regions had emerged in the English Colonies: New England, the Middle Colonies, and the South. Because of differences in topography and climate, different ways of life emerged in each of these three regions. This, in turn, attracted different types of people, reinforcing differences in physical geography. Differences among these regions, especially between the North and the South, led directly to the sectionalism of the early 19th century and later to the outbreak of the Civil War.

HUMAN-ENVIRONMENT INTERACTION

People shape their environment and are shaped by it. The location of key natural resources and natural transportation routes dictated the location of cities and industries. For example, major cities emerged at the hubs of several transportation routes, especially along the Atlantic seaboard and the Great Lakes. People also shaped their environment. The arrival of settlers further transformed the American landscape from forests and rolling plains to farms, towns, and cities.

Library of Congress

As settlers moved into an area, they shaped the landscape by clearing it and building homes

MOVEMENT

Movement of people, goods and even ideas from one place to another often has important consequences. The arrival of Europeans to the Americas had a great impact on the Native American Indians and on the geography and wildlife of the region. Gradually, European exploration and settlement moved from the Atlantic coastline westwards, eventually reaching the Pacific Ocean.

MAJOR HISTORICAL DEVELOPMENTS

THE FIRST AMERICANS

More than twenty thousand years ago, human beings first went from Asia to the Americas by crossing the narrow land bridge that once connected Siberia and Alaska. They were hunters and gatherers, moving from place to place in search of food. From Alaska, these peoples slowly spread southwards

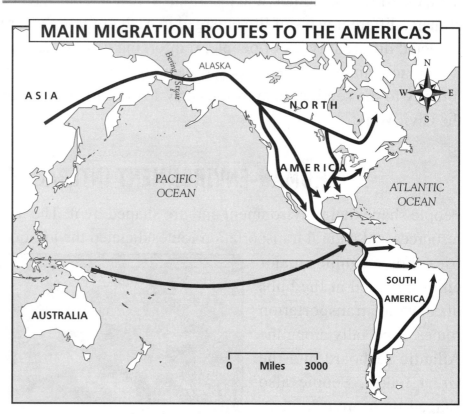

into North and South America. Now known as **Native American Indians,** they developed different lifestyles depending upon the resources and climates that they found.

THE RISE OF NATIVE AMERICAN EMPIRES

In Mexico, Central America, and South America, Native American peoples created highly developed societies. The **Maya** developed the earliest Native American Indian civilization. Located in southern Mexico and Guatemala, the Maya made discoveries in science, astronomy, and mathematics. The **Aztecs** created an empire in central Mexico about 700 years ago. They built stoneworks, pyramids, and temples. Along the Andes Mountains in South America, the **Incas** also formed a large empire, with extensive roads to connect their territories.

THE NEW YORK CONNECTION

The earliest Native American Indians in New York were the Algonquians. Iroquois tribes, also known as the Haudenosaunee (*the people of the long-house*), later settled in northwestern New York.

LIFESTYLES

Native American Indian peoples adapted to the environment in which they settled. Algonquians lived in **wigwams** (*round houses made of branches, bark, and grass*). Iroquois families lived together in **longhouses** — long rectangular shelters (*also made of branches, bark, and grass*).

The interior of a longhouse

New York State Archives

Algonquian and Iroquois men hunted and fished, and were fierce warriors. Women were responsible for growing corn and squash and preparing food. The Algonquians and Iroquois tribes made clothes from the skins of deer and other animals they hunted.

THE IROQUOIS CONFEDERACY

The five Iroquois tribes (*Cayuga, Mohawk, Onondaga, Oneida, and Seneca*) formed the **Iroquois Confederacy** in 1570. A hundred years later, a sixth tribe, the Tuscarora, joined. This early form of political union had its own constitution, in which Iroquois tribes promised not to fight one another. It is believed the Iroquois constitution later influenced some authors of the U.S. Constitution.

EUROPEANS EXPLORE THE AMERICAS

About 500 years ago, better navigational skills and technological advances like the compass and astrolabe made it possible for Europeans to sail farther than ever before. Gunpowder made it possible for them to create strong armies. Strong rulers sought to find new trade routes to Asia, while missionaries sought to spread Christianity. These factors led Europeans to explore the oceans.

Christopher Columbus (1451–1506), an Italian navigator, believed he could reach China and the Spice Islands by sailing westwards. Columbus set sail in 1492. He landed in the West Indies, where he later established Spain's first settlement in the New World. Other explorers, missionaries, and colonists soon followed Columbus. Europeans learned about new foods and obtained gold, silver, and land. Native American Indians were easily conquered by Europeans, who had such weapons as guns, cannons, and horses. Meanwhile, European diseases dramatically reduced Native American Indian populations.

EUROPEAN COLONIAL EMPIRES

Spain's empire in the New World increased the interest of its rivals, France, Holland, and England. Each sent its own explorers to claim lands in the Americas and find a **Northwest Passage** to Asia. French explorers **Jacques Cartier, Samuel de Champlain,** and **Robert de la LaSalle** explored the St. Lawrence River, Great Lakes, and Mississippi River. **New France** was established in Canada.

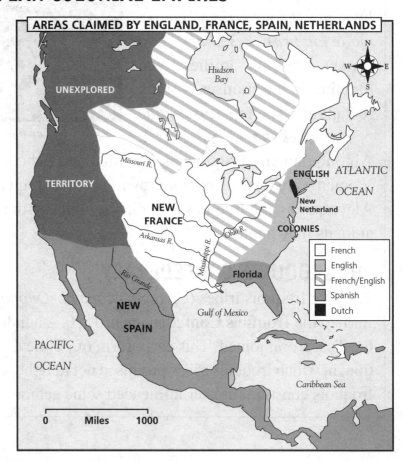

AREAS CLAIMED BY ENGLAND, FRANCE, SPAIN, NETHERLANDS

The first English colony was started at Jamestown, Virginia, in 1607. Soon, the colony at Jamestown became profitable by growing tobacco for sale in Europe. Meanwhile, Pilgrims and Puritans established colonies in Massachusetts, in order to practice their religion freely.

In the **Mayflower Compact** (1620), the Pilgrims, while crossing the Atlantic, agreed to form their own colonial government and to obey its laws. This new government based its powers from the consent of the governed.

THE NEW YORK CONNECTION

Based on the explorations of **Henry Hudson** in 1609, the Dutch established a colony which they called **New Netherland.** They built a settlement at **Fort Orange** (*now Albany*) and **New Amsterdam** (*now Manhattan*). Most early colonists tended to settle near rivers where they had an adequate source of water for raising crops. These early colonies were governed by the **Dutch West India Company.** The company appointed a governor in order to control the colony. The most famous governor was **Peter Stuyvesant.**

New Netherland separated the English colonies north and south of it. In 1664, Stuyvesant surrendered the colony to English forces. New Netherland became an English colony and was renamed **New York.** New Amsterdam became **New York City** and Fort Orange was renamed **Albany.**

THE ENGLISH COLONIES

By the mid-1730s, the thirteen English colonies had spread up and down the Atlantic coast. Colonial communities developed along European patterns. English colonists enjoyed the same rights as people living in England. The economy of the colonies was based on **mercantilism.** When put into practice, mercantilism was meant to increase a nation's wealth, and with it, its power. Under this policy, the colonists were expected to sell their raw materials, such as tobacco, rice, indigo, and fish at a low price to Britain. In exchange, the colonists were counted on to buy more expensive British manufactured products — glass, china, and books.

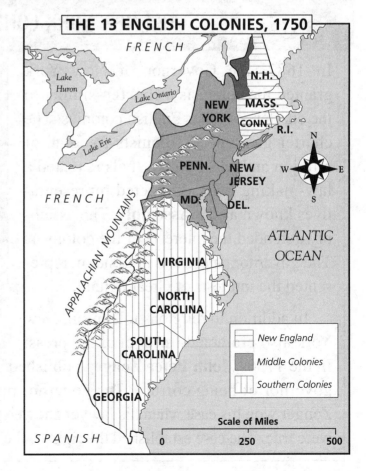

THE 13 ENGLISH COLONIES, 1750

FRENCH
Lake Huron
Lake Ontario
Lake Erie
FRENCH
APPALACHIAN MOUNTAINS
N.H.
NEW YORK
MASS.
CONN.
R.I.
PENN.
NEW JERSEY
MD.
DEL.
VIRGINIA
NORTH CAROLINA
SOUTH CAROLINA
GEORGIA
ATLANTIC OCEAN
SPANISH

New England
Middle Colonies
Southern Colonies

Scale of Miles
0   250   500

Different economic patterns of life developed in three separate regions:

NEW ENGLAND

The colonies of New England — Massachusetts, New Hampshire, Connecticut and Rhode Island — had less fertile land and a colder climate than the other colonies. New Englanders had small farms where they grew crops for their own use. Many people from this area chose occupations as sailors, merchants, or fishermen. Some became involved in a **Triangular Trade** — trading rum for African slaves and slaves for Caribbean molasses.

THE MIDDLE COLONIES

The Middle Colonies of New York, New Jersey, Delaware, Pennsylvania, and Maryland were located between New England and the Southern Colonies. Winters were not as harsh as in New England and summers were longer. Uncleared forests and fertile soils helped to draw many settlers to this area. People were also attracted to these colonies by the atmosphere of religious freedom.

 THE NEW YORK CONNECTION

In 1682, the Governor of New York granted the colonists a **charter,** similar to the charters of other English colonies. The charter guaranteed colonists freedom of religion and trial by jury. It also created a law-making body of elected representatives known as the **Assembly.** The assembly defended the interests of the colonists. The governor, appointed in London, represented the interests of Great Britain.

British soldiers burn copies of
John Peter Zenger's Weekley Journal

Library of Congress

In addition to religious toleration, New York also promoted freedom of the press. In the 1730s, **John Peter Zenger** published a newspaper which accused the governor of being corrupt. The governor put Zenger on trial for libel, but Zenger won his case when his lawyer showed that the statements he published were true. The case established the right of the press to criticize those in power.

THE SOUTHERN COLONIES

The climate of the Southern Colonies — Virginia, Maryland, North Carolina, South Carolina, and Georgia — was warmer than other parts of colonial America. The soil was well-suited to growing crops. Some Southerners developed large plantations which grew tobacco, cotton, rice, and indigo (*blue dye*) for shipment to England in exchange for manufactured goods. Most of the larger plantations used enslaved peoples from Africa, and their descendants, as the main work force.

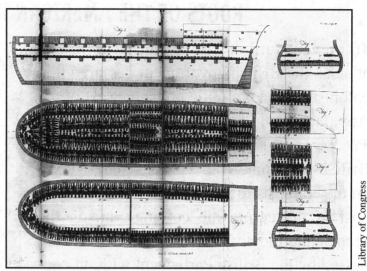

About 20 million Africans were inhumanely packed in slave ships and taken across the Atlantic

THE ROAD TO INDEPENDENCE

THE FRENCH AND INDIAN WAR, 1754–1763

By the 1750s, the British claimed control of the Ohio River Valley, just across the Appalachians. The French had built forts along the St. Lawrence River and the Great Lakes to keep British fur traders and settlers from crossing into their lands, and also claimed the Ohio River Valley.

War between Britain and France finally broke out in 1754. Because many Native American Indian tribes sided with the French, the contest in North America became known as the **French and Indian War.** Delegations from the colonies met at Albany to discuss common plans for defense. Benjamin Franklin proposed a plan for a central colonial government that would share power with the separate colonies. However, this **Albany Plan of Union** found no support from the colonial assemblies.

A British force captured Quebec in 1759, giving Britain control of the St. Lawrence River. Under the terms of the **Treaty of Paris** (1763), France lost much of its colonial empire in North America — Canada and all lands east of the Mississippi River — to the British.

ROOTS OF THE AMERICAN REVOLUTION

To prevent further Native American Indian attacks, the British government declared that colonists could not settle on lands west of the Appalachians. The **Proclamation Line of 1763** was resented by many colonists. The British government also proposed new taxes on the colonists to help pay off debts from the cost of protecting the colonies during the French and Indian War. A series of taxes were passed by the British Parliament without consulting the colonists. The colonists protested, arguing that such "taxation without representation" was tyranny. They particularly objected to the **Stamp Act** (1765), which taxed newspapers and official documents. This tax created a firestorm of protest in the colonies. Colonists **boycotted** (*refused to buy*) British goods as a form of protest.

Colonists burn seized stamped newspapers to protest the tax

In response to these protests, the British canceled almost all of the new taxes except for the tariff on tea. In 1773, some colonists protested against the tea tax by dumping British tea into Boston harbor. The **"Boston Tea Party"** brought a strong reaction from the British govern-

Colonists disguised as Native American Indians dump British tea into Boston harbor

ment. It closed Boston harbor and restricted the freedom of citizens in Massachusetts, greatly increasing tensions between the colonists and Great Britain.

THE REVOLUTION BEGINS

Colonists had already learned the value of cooperation during the French and Indian War. Representatives from the colonies met in Philadelphia to discuss common concerns. This **First Continental Congress** decided to continue protesting British taxes. In 1775, open warfare broke out between British soldiers and colonists at Concord, Massachusetts. The fighting quickly spread to other colonies and marked the start of the **American Revolutionary War.** The British sent more troops to America to put down the colonial rebellion.

THE DECLARATION OF INDEPENDENCE

A variety of viewpoints developed in response to the outbreak of war. **Loyalists** wanted to remain under British rule. **Patriots** wanted independence. In 1776, representatives from all 13 colonies met again in Philadelphia for the **Second Continental Congress.** After much debate, the delegates decided to declare American independence from Britain.

Library of Congress

Thomas Jefferson led a committee to write the **Declaration of Independence.** This document, issued on **July 4, 1776.** Its primary purpose was to explain the reasons why the colonists should be independent from Great Britain. Influenced by English thinkers like **John Locke,** Jefferson believed that government was a "social contract," and that citizens had a right to overthrow an oppressive government. The Declaration stated:

Jefferson meets with the committee assigned to help him write the Declaration of Independence

"We hold these truths to be self-evident, that all men are created equal, that they are endowed by their Creator with certain Unalienable Rights, that among these are Life, Liberty and the pursuit of Happiness. That to secure these rights, Governments are instituted among Men, deriving their just powers from the consent of the governed, That whenever any Form of Government becomes destructive of these ends, it is the right of the People to alter or abolish it, and to institute new Government..."

THE BATTLE FOR INDEPENDENCE, 1775–1783

In the first years of the war, the colonial army barely managed to escape from one disaster after another. Under General **George Washington,** the colonists lost several early key battles in New Jersey and New York, but managed to keep their forces intact.

THE NEW YORK CONNECTION

During the revolution, more fighting took place in New York than in any other colony. The colonists, led by **Ethan Allen,** captured **Fort Ticonderoga** in 1775. George Washington and the Continental Army occupied New York City in 1776. Despite these successes, the British drove Washington and his army out of New York after the **Battle of Long Island.** British troops then occupied New York City. In 1777, the English had a plan to win the war by dividing the colonies through New York. The plan failed when their army, commanded by General **John Burgoyne,** was defeated at Saratoga, New York by General **Horatio Gates.** The **Battle of Saratoga** (1777) was the turning point in the war. The British strategy to divide the colonies was now in shambles.

The victory at Saratoga helped convince France to supply military assistance to the Americans. With French help, Washington managed to force the British to surrender at the **Battle of Yorktown** in Virginia in 1781. Under the terms of the Treaty of Paris (1783), the British recognized American independence and gave the lands between the Mississippi River and the Atlantic coast from the

British General Burgoyne surrenders to General Gates after the Battle of Saratoga

Great Lakes to Florida, to the new United States. In New York, the victory over the British led to the collapse of the Iroquois Confederacy, which had mainly sided with the British. In addition, many Loyalists fled to Canada. American soldiers who fought in the Revolution were rewarded with farmland in Northern and Western New York.

SUMMARIZING YOUR UNDERSTANDING

Each content chapter concludes with a *Summarizing Your Understanding*, which identifies an overarching theme highlighting a key generalization in the chapter. Key terms, concepts and people in the chapter are also listed.

OVERARCHING THEME

The geography of an area often affects the settlement patterns and living conditions of its people.

KEY TERMS, CONCEPTS, AND PEOPLE

★ Maya, Aztec, and Inca Empires

★ French and Indian War

★ Albany Plan of Union

★ Stamp Act

★ Boston Tea Party

★ American Revolutionary War

★ Declaration of Independence

★ Battle of Saratoga

TESTING YOUR UNDERSTANDING

MULTIPLE-CHOICE QUESTIONS

1   **The Iroquois and Algonquians are names that would most likely appear in an essay discussing**
   1   famous American inventions
   2   Native American Indian tribes
   3   European explorers
   4   colonial religious beliefs

2   **The Cayuga, Onondaga, and Mohawk were all members of the**
   1   Albany Plan of Union
   2   Iroquois Confederation
   3   Colonial Assemblies
   4   Mayflower Compact

3 **The emergence of "New England," "New France," "New Spain," and "New Netherland" in the Americas shows the**
  1   limits of political power in Europe
  2   spread of Native American Indian empires
  3   influence of European settlement in North and South America
  4   expansion of European power in Asia

4 **A primary source of information about New Amsterdam would be**
  1   a history of the United States
  2   a television show about the British colonies
  3   a diary written by Peter Stuyvesant
  4   an interview with a historian on the Colonial Period

5 **People living in the thirteen colonies adopted many of their principles of government from**
  1   Portugal   3   Great Britain
  2   Spain   4   France

Base your answers to questions 6 and 7 on the map below.

6 **What type of goods were shipped from England to the colonies?**
  1   slaves, gold, and pepper
  2   sugar and molasses
  3   manufactured goods
  4   rum and iron

7 **This map deals mainly with which aspect of colonial life?**
  1   political
  2   social
  3   economic
  4   religious

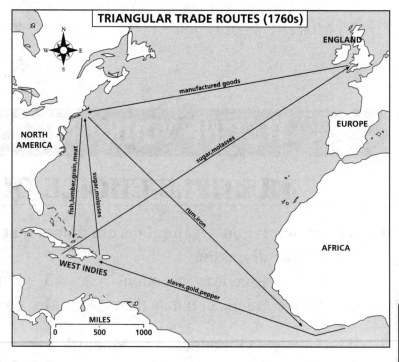

8   During the colonial era, the creation of colonial assemblies represented
1   attempts to build a strong national government
2   British efforts to strengthen their control over the colonies
3   a step in the growth of representative democracy
4   the sharing of power by the national and state governments

9   Which event led to the other three?
1   issuance of the Declaration of Independence
2   meeting of the First Continental Congress
3   the Boston Tea Party
4   new British tax policies after the French and Indian War

10   What was the main purpose of the Stamp Act?
1   to organize the first colonial post office
2   to raise money to pay the salary of colonial assemblies
3   to raise money to repay British costs for the French and Indian War
4   to guarantee that all colonies would pay the same for a stamp

11   "Taxation without representation" was a response by the colonists to
1   sharing tax monies with Native American Indian tribes
2   a provision in the Treaty of Paris of 1783
3   British economic policies towards the colonies
4   the formation of the Iroquois Confederacy

12   The major purpose of the Declaration of Independence was to
1   establish the basic laws of the United States
2   justify the revolt of the American colonists against Great Britain
3   provide a clear plan for a new government
4   call for the creation of new state governments

13   Which action could be justified by ideas expressed in the Declaration of Independence?
1   A democratic government cracks down on terrorists.
2   Citizens try to overthrow an oppressive government.
3   The government releases political prisoners.
4   A government passes laws to segregate different races.

14 **The capture of Fort Ticonderoga, the Battle of Long Island, and the Battle of Saratoga would be found in a book dealing with**

   1   famous Maya and Inca battles

   2   Dutch rule in New Amsterdam

   3   the French and Indian War

   4   the American Revolutionary War

CONSTRUCTED-RESPONSE QUESTIONS

Base your answers to questions 1 through 3 on the line graph below and your knowledge of Social Studies.

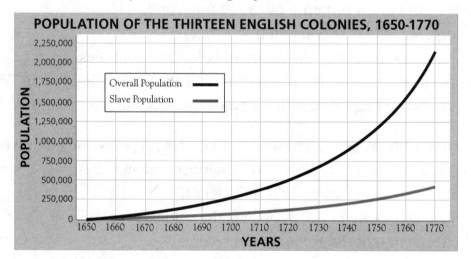

POPULATION OF THE THIRTEEN ENGLISH COLONIES, 1650-1770

1. What was the population of the thirteen English colonies in 1730? _____

_____

2. Which had a greater growth rate between 1750 and 1770: the total population of the colonies or the slave population? _____

_____

3. What trend does this graph illustrate about the population of the thirteen English colonies after 1720? _____

_____

_____

DOCUMENT-BASED QUESTIONS: READING AND INTERPRETING DOCUMENTS

> The **Grade 8 Intermediate Social Studies Test** will require you to answer a document-based question. To help you answer such a question, you will find a *Document-Based Questions* section at the end of each content chapter.

READING HISTORICAL DOCUMENTS

THE SEARCH FOR MEANING

Most document-based questions on the test will present short reading passages of a few sentences. These passages will often be excerpts (*parts*) of a longer speech or writing. When you read a historical document, it is helpful to imagine yourself back in time in order to understand the author's point of view. People in the past often had very different attitudes and concerns than we have today. In reading a historical document, you need to be a critical reader. It helps if you know something about the writer's background, in order to understand how it affected his or her ideas. Below are some important questions you should ask yourself when reading a historical document or passage:

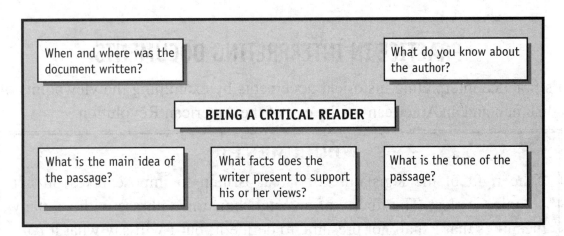

When and where was the document written?

What do you know about the author?

BEING A CRITICAL READER

What is the main idea of the passage?

What facts does the writer present to support his or her views?

What is the tone of the passage?

Sometimes you will not know who the author of a historical document was. This may be the case if the document is a flyer, broadside, newspaper article, or pamphlet. Think about who would have read the flyer or article, and what the purpose of the document might have been. For example, if the document is an advertisement, its purpose is to persuade readers to buy something. The advertisement will probably say good things about the product, and avoid saying bad things.

DETERMINING WORD MEANINGS FROM CONTEXT CLUES

Often you will come across an unfamiliar word or phrase in a document. **Context clues** can help you figure out what they mean. Think of yourself as a detective. The surrounding words, phrases and sentences provide clues to help you uncover the meaning of the unfamiliar word.

Part of Speech. From the words in the sentence, can you guess what part of speech the unfamiliar word is? Is it a noun, verb, or some other part of speech?

Substitute Words. Can you guess the meaning of the word from the tone or meaning of the rest of the passage? What other words would make sense if you substituted them in place of the unfamiliar word?

USING CONTEXT CLUES TO FIND THE MEANING

Related Familiar Words. Is the word similar to another word you already know? Does it help you to figure out what the word means? Can you make out what the word is by breaking it up into parts — such as a prefix, root, or suffix?

Bypass the Word. Can you understand the main idea of the sentence without knowing the meaning of the unfamiliar word? If so, it may not be important to spend time trying to figure out its meaning.

PRACTICE IN INTERPRETING DOCUMENTS

Let's practice interpreting historical documents by examining the viewpoints of an Englishman and an American on the eve of the American Revolution.

DOCUMENT 1

"The right of the legislature of Great Britain to impose taxes on her colonies is clear. The liberty of an Englishman is a phrase with so many meanings that I shall not presume to define it; but I will say what it *cannot* mean, which is an *exemption* from taxes imposed by the Parliament of Great Britain. Nor is there any charter that ever pretended to grant such a privilege to any colony in America."

— *Soame Jenyns, a Member of the Parliament of Great Britain, 1765*

Suppose you did not understand the word *exemption* in the middle of document. Below is a method for figuring out the meaning of this word.

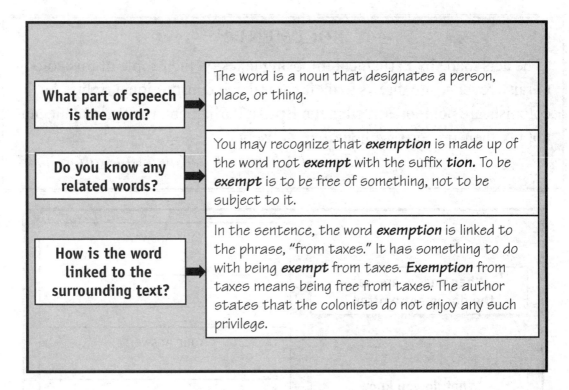

Now let's look at the document as a whole. Consider the background of the author and what the author is trying to say in this document.

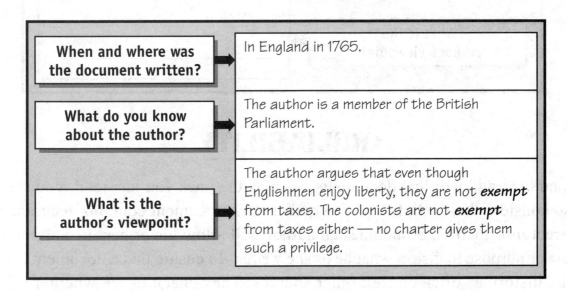

Now that you finished interpreting **Document 1,** compare Soame Jenyn's views with a second opinion about taxation — that of an American colonist.

DOCUMENT 2

"The acts made by Parliament imposing taxes on the people of this colony to raise revenue are threats to their natural and constitutional rights. As the colonists are not represented in the British Parliament, the Parliament cannot tax their property without their consent."

— *Samuel Adams, a letter against taxation, 1767*

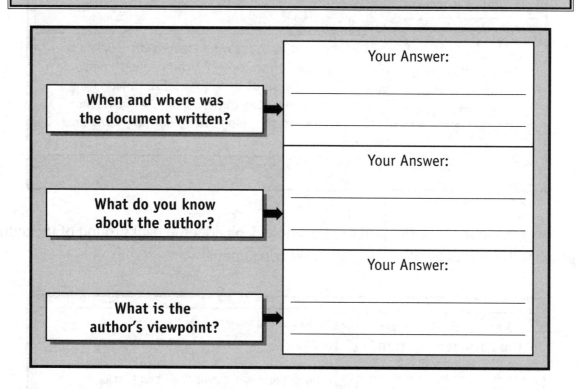

When and where was the document written?

Your Answer:
_____
_____

What do you know about the author?

Your Answer:
_____
_____

What is the author's viewpoint?

Your Answer:
_____
_____

RELIABILITY

When reading historical documents, such as the ones you just read, you should also consider their **reliability** — whether each document contains accurate and correct information. Sometimes an author will allow his or her special point of view or purpose to distort what he or she writes. To ensure that a document is reliable, historians often consult other sources. They check to see whether all the facts about an event were reported accurately or whether important details have been omitted from the account. They also check to see if the author is just giving opinions or providing facts to support his or her view.

CHAPTER 6

THE NEW NATION: BIRTH AND GROWTH, From 1783 to 1840

In this chapter, you will learn how Americans first governed themselves after achieving independence from Great Britain. In addition, you will read about the new U.S. Constitution and some of the important compromises that took place in writing that document. As you read this chapter, you will learn about:

The rotunda at the National Archives where the U.S. Constitution is on permanent exhibit

National Archives

★ **The Articles of Confederation.** Under the Articles of Confederation, most government powers were left to the states. This system of government proved too weak to handle the problems facing the nation.

★ **The U.S. Constitution.** To correct problems existing under the Articles of Confederation, a new Constitution was written in 1787.

★ **The New Government in Operation.** Presidents Washington, Jefferson and Jackson established important traditions that allowed the new nation to develop and prosper.

In studying this period, you should focus on the following questions:

★ What accomplishments and problems did Americans experience under the Articles of Confederation?

★ How did the U.S. Constitution establish a strong national government without threatening individual liberties?

★ What problems did early American Presidents face?

MAJOR THEMES IN U.S. HISTORY: GOVERNMENT

WHAT IS GOVERNMENT?

People are social beings. They cannot survive and prosper unless they live together in groups or communities. Communities in turn need rules about how their members should behave to maintain peace and order. They also need some authority to enforce the rules and settle disputes. The organization set up to protect the community and enforce its rules is known as **government.** The members of a community are known as its **citizens;** they have responsibilities as well as rights in a well-governed society.

THE POWERS OF GOVERNMENT

All governments have three special powers.

> a **legislative power** to make laws

> an **executive power** to carry out the laws

> a **judicial power** to apply and interpret the laws

In this chapter, you will learn how the citizens of America created a stable form of democratic government after achieving their independence from Great Britain. They wanted the United States to be a **republic** — a country with a government chosen by the people. Americans experimented with their form of government before finally drafting the U.S. Constitution in 1787. That Constitution still provides the basis for the American form of government today.

National Archives

The signing of the U.S. Constitution at Independence Hall, September 17, 1787

MAJOR HISTORICAL DEVELOPMENTS

THE ARTICLES OF CONFEDERATION: THE NATION'S FIRST GOVERNMENT

After winning independence, each former colony became an independent state. Colonial charters were rewritten as state constitutions.

THE NEW YORK CONNECTION

A convention of New Yorkers met in White Plains and Kingston to write a state constitution in 1777. The constitution was adopted by the convention without being voted on by most New Yorkers. It created a government similar in some ways to the colonial government. There was a governor with a three-year term, a system of state courts, and a new legislature consisting of the Senate and Assembly. The new state constitution also included the Declaration of Independence. Based on democratic principles, it gave adult male property owners the right to vote. It also required voters to decide whether to revise the constitution every 20 years. New York's constitution was important to governing New York State and later the nation. In 1787, it served as one of the models for the U.S. Constitution.

George Clinton,
New York's first governor

The former colonists realized the need for some form of central, or national, government. Because of their experience with British rule, however, they were afraid of creating a central government that would be too powerful. In 1781, the new states adopted the **Articles of Confederation.** This agreement created a weak central government in which the state governments could cooperate. Each state sent one representative to the new Congress. Congress could declare war and settle disputes, but it could not collect its own taxes or raise its own army. There was no President or national court system.

ACHIEVEMENTS AND PROBLEMS

The Confederation Congress signed the peace treaty with Britain, ending the American Revolution. The Confederation Congress also passed the **Northwest Ordinance of 1787,** which set up procedures for the eventual admission of territories in the Northwest Territory as new states once their populations increased.

THE NORTHWEST TERRITORY

Lake Superior

UPPER CANADA
(British territory)

Lake Huron

(Wisconsin)
1848

Lake Ontario

N.Y.

Mississippi R.

(Michigan)
1837

Lake Erie

PENN.

SPANISH
LOUISIANA

(Illinois)
1818

(Indiana)
1816

(Ohio)
1803

Ohio R.

VIRGINIA

Dates = year
admitted to Union

KENTUCKY

N. CAROLINA

Some Americans feared that the new government had too little power to do its job properly. When an uprising of farmers — known as **Shays' Rebellion** — broke out in Massachusetts in 1786, there was no national army to put it down if it spread to other states. Although the state militia was able to put down the rebellion, many Americans now saw the need for a stronger national government.

THE NATION GETS A NEW CONSTITUTION

In 1787, representatives from the states met in Philadelphia to revise the Articles of Confederation. The representatives quickly decided that a new national constitution was needed. They further agreed that the new national government should have the power to collect taxes and raise an army, and should have a President, a legislature (*Congress*) and a court system.

In this room delegates wrote the U.S. Constitution

Eastern National Park & Monument Assoc.

There were also several disagreements among the delegates that were eventually settled by compromise. Two of the most important concerned representation and slavery.

MAJOR CONSITUTIONAL COMPROMISES

Issue: How should states be represented in the national legislature?

Issue: How should slaves be counted?

The "Great Compromise:" Larger states felt they should have a greater say in the national government. Smaller states felt each state should have an equal voice. In this compromise, two "houses" were created in the legislature (*Congress*). In the House of Representatives, states were represented according to their population size. This allowed states with a larger population to have a greater number of representatives. In the Senate, each state, no matter what its size, would be represented by two Senators. All laws needed the approval of both houses of Congress.

The "Three-Fifths Compromise:" Southern states wanted slaves counted as part of their population, to have more members in the House of Representatives. The states compromised by agreeing to count every five slaves as three free persons for both taxation and representation.

FREE PERSONS = SLAVES

TAXATION AND REPRESENTATION

CONSTITUTIONAL PRINCIPLES

The representatives who met in 1787 agreed on the **core values** of the American democratic system. They supported representative government, equality and justice — even if they did not recognize the need to apply these ideas to women, slaves, and several other groups.

The basic challenge faced by the authors of the U.S. Constitution was to create a national government that would be strong, but not so strong that it would undermine individual liberties. To achieve this goal, the new Constitution adopted a number of important principles:

★ **Democracy.** Our Constitution is based on democracy. Americans decide, through their elected representatives, what the government should do. This principle is stated in the **Preamble** of the Constitution, "We the People ..." It tells us that under our form of government it is the *people* who *hold the real power.* The **majority** makes decisions, although they also respect **minority rights.**

★ **Federalism.** The writers of the Constitution created a system where power was shared between the national government and the state governments. In this division of power, the national government deals with matters that affect the whole country. State governments handle their own local affairs. Each American is a **citizen** both of his or her own state, and of the nation as whole.

★ **Separation of Powers.** The authors of the Constitution feared leaving too much power to any one branch of government. As a result, they separated the main powers of the central government — **legislative, executive, and judicial powers** — into different branches: **Congress,** the **President,** and the **Supreme Court** (*and other federal courts*).

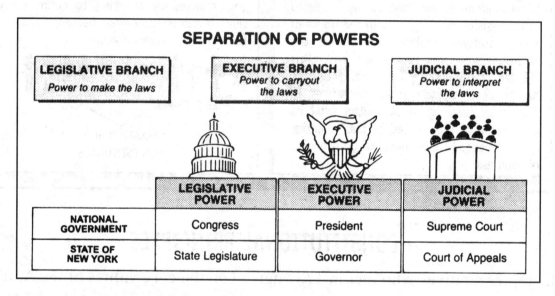

SEPARATION OF POWERS

LEGISLATIVE BRANCH Power to make the laws	**EXECUTIVE BRANCH** Power to carryout the laws	**JUDICIAL BRANCH** Power to interpret the laws

	LEGISLATIVE POWER	**EXECUTIVE POWER**	**JUDICIAL POWER**
NATIONAL GOVERNMENT	Congress	President	Supreme Court
STATE OF NEW YORK	State Legislature	Governor	Court of Appeals

★ **Checks and Balances.** To prevent any one of the three branches from becoming too powerful, the Constitution gave each branch ways to stop or "check" the other branches. For example, the Senate must approve most Presidential appointments. In this way, power was "balanced" so that many actions cannot be taken without some more general agreement.

★ **Ability to Change.** Although over 200 years old, the Constitution has kept up with the changing needs of the nation. The **elastic clause** and changing interpretations by the Supreme Court have helped adapt the Constitution to new conditions. The Constitution also keeps pace through the **amendment** process — additions to the Constitution. To prevent changes except for very important reasons and with widespread agreement, the amending process was made far more difficult than the process for passing an ordinary law.

THE STATES DEBATE RATIFICATION

The members of the Constitutional Convention knew that they could not adopt their new plan of government on their own authority. They decided that before the Constitution could become law, nine states would have to ratify (*approve*) it. Special conventions were held in each state for this purpose.

FEDERALISTS AND ANTI-FEDERALISTS

Opponents of the new Constitution, called **Anti-Federalists,** believed it would create a strong central government that would threaten individual freedom. They feared future government leaders might build a strong army and use it to collect unpopular taxes. Anti-Federalists also pointed out that there was no bill of rights in the new Constitution to protect individual liberties.

Those favoring the proposed Constitution were called **Federalists.** They pointed out that government under the Articles of Confederation had broken down. They argued that a stronger central government was needed to preserve political independence. They also argued that under the proposed plan, federalism and the separation of powers would prevent any one branch of the new government from becoming too strong.

James Madison, another contributor to The Federalist Papers, was instrumental in getting the new Constitution approved

THE NEW YORK CONNECTION

New Yorkers played an important role in getting the new constitution adopted. New Yorkers **Alexander Hamilton** and **John Jay** contributed to *The Federalist Papers,* a series of essays that argued that the new nation would not last long if the proposed constitution were not adopted. These essays helped to convince New Yorkers and other Americans to approve the new constitution.

THE RATIFICATION PROCESS

By the end of 1788, twelve states had voted to **ratify** (*approve*) the Constitution. In several states, support was won only by promising that a **Bill of Rights** would be added. A Bill of Rights was added to the Constitution in 1791 in the form of the first ten amendments. These ten amendments protect important individual liberties:

1. *Guarantees the freedoms of religion, speech, the press, and assembly.*
2. *Guarantees the right to keep and bear arms.*
3. *Prohibits the forcible quartering of soldiers in one's home.*
4. *Prohibits unreasonable searches and seizures.*
5. *Guarantees that no citizen can be deprived of life, liberty or property without* **due process of law** *(procedures according to established rules, such as a fair trial); also prohibits* **double jeopardy** *(being tried twice for the same crime) and* **self-incrimination** *(no person can be forced to give evidence against himself).*
6. *Guarantees those accused of a crime the right to a speedy trial by jury, to confront their accusers, and to be represented by a lawyer.*
7. *Guarantees a jury trial in many civil cases.*
8. *Prohibits excessive bail and cruel and unusual punishment.*
9. *States that the listing of some rights in the Constitution does not mean that people do not also enjoy other rights.*
10. *Reserves for the states and the people those powers not given to the federal government, forming a basis for the reserved powers.*

For example, the First Amendment guarantees the separation of church and state as well as an individual's freedom of speech. It also guarantees the exchange of ideas through freedom of the press.

THE NEW GOVERNMENT IN OPERATION

THE PRESIDENCY OF GEORGE WASHINGTON, 1789–1797

In 1789 in New York City, George Washington was inaugurated as the first President of the United States. His major challenge was to provide stability and civility to the nation under its new form of government. The world was watching to see if this new experiment in democracy would survive: could ordinary citizens participate actively in a democratic government, and reach decisions peacefully without armed conflict?

Domestic policy refers to government policies that deal with conditions within the nation. **Foreign policy** concerns relations with other countries.

WASHINGTON'S DOMESTIC POLICY

Forming a Government. The Constitution allowed the President to appoint officials to be in charge of executive departments. The chief officials that Washington appointed also began meeting with him in what came to be known as the **Cabinet.** Over the years, as the government assumed greater responsibilities, new Cabinet departments were created.

Raising Money. Washington next turned his attention to the large debt left from fighting the American Revolutionary War. The job of solving the nation's economic problems went to **Alexander Hamilton,** the Secretary of the Treasury. Hamilton drew up a four-part program for getting the nation on a sound financial basis:

Library of Congress

President Washington (far right) meets with his Cabinet

HAMILTON'S FINANCIAL PLAN

| **Repay the Debt.** Hamilton believed the national government should pay off the debts of both the states and the previous national government in order to establish the nation's credit. | **National Bank.** Hamilton proposed creation of a national bank as a place to deposit taxes, to provide a sound currency, and to make loans to the national government. | **Whiskey Tax.** Hamilton proposed a tax on whiskey to raise money from western farmers. | **Protective Tariff.** Hamilton asked Congress to pass a high tariff — a tax on imported foreign goods which would protect American industries from foreign competition. |

The Rise of Political Parties. Hamilton's program was strongly opposed by Thomas Jefferson, Washington's Secretary of State. Jefferson and his followers believed Hamilton's plan would benefit only the wealthy while hurting most others. This disagreement led to the development of America's first **political parties** — groups that try to elect their members to government offices so that they can pass laws favorable to their ideas. Hamilton's followers became known as **Federalists;** Jefferson's supporters called themselves **Democratic-Republicans.** The Cabinet, political parties, and other practices that have developed (*like the formation of Congressional Committees*) are often referred to as the **unwritten Constitution.**

Thomas Jefferson

Library of Congress

Defeat of the Protective Tariff. All of Hamilton's program was approved except for the proposed tariff. Southern states opposed the tariff because they believed it would make it harder for them to sell their crops to Britain and to buy British goods.

The Whiskey Rebellion of 1794. Farmers living west of the Appalachian Mountains often converted their excess grain into whiskey. Western farmers did this because it was easier to transport whiskey over the mountains than bushels of grain. The new federal whiskey tax caused hostility among these farmers. When they refused to pay the tax, Washington called up the militia and put down the rebellion.

WASHINGTON'S FOREIGN POLICY

The new nation was weak militarily. A revolution in France led to war between France and Britain in 1793. Jefferson's supporters favored the French revolutionaries, while the Federalists favored the British.

The Proclamation of Neutrality (1793). To prevent being drawn into the conflict, Washington adopted a policy of **neutrality:** the United States would avoid taking sides in European disputes or becoming involved in foreign wars.

Washington's Farewell Address. After two terms in office, Washington declined to serve a third time. In 1796, Washington delivered his **Farewell Address** to Congress. In this speech, he encouraged commercial ties with foreign countries, but cautioned Americans against entering into permanent political alliances.

THE PRESIDENCY OF THOMAS JEFFERSON, 1801–1809

The next President, **John Adams** (1797–1801), was a Federalist who continued Washington's policies. In 1800, Adams lost the election to Thomas Jefferson.

JEFFERSON'S VIEWS ON GOVERNMENT

Jefferson saw his election as a turning point for the nation. He believed the best government was a weak one. Jefferson opposed special privileges for the wealthy, and had strong sympathies for the common farmer. As President, he set about reducing the size of the army, ending naval expansion, and lowering government costs.

THE LOUISIANA PURCHASE (1803)

In 1803, **Napoleon Bonaparte,** ruler of France, offered to sell the **Louisiana Territory** to the United States. Although uncertain if the Constitution allowed the federal government to buy new territory, Jefferson went ahead with the purchase. The Louisiana Territory doubled the size of the nation. Jefferson appointed **Meriwether Lewis** and **William Clark** to explore and map the region.

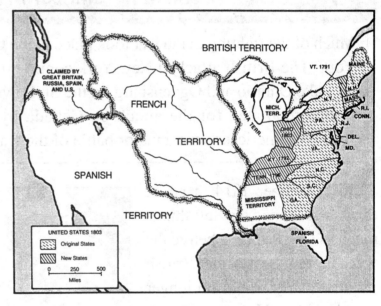

EMBARGO ACT OF 1807

With war raging between Britain and France, British ships began stopping U.S. ships to search for deserters from the British navy. This practice humiliated Americans and put pressure on Jefferson to take action. To avoid war, Jefferson pushed the **Embargo Act** through Congress. American ships were prohibited from trading with European nations. The act hurt the U.S. economy and led to a depression.

During Jefferson's Presidency, the Supreme Court established its right of **judicial review.** Using judicial review, the court declared its power to interpret the U.S Constitution and to decide whether or not a law is constitutional.

PRESERVING THE NATION'S INDEPENDENCE

After only thirty years of independence, Americans were drawn into a second war.

THE OUTBREAK OF THE WAR OF 1812

During their war with France, British ships stopped American ships and **impressed** (*seized*) U.S. sailors, claiming they were deserters from the British navy. Meanwhile, some Americans thought the time was ripe to seize Canada from the British. In 1812, Congress declared war on Britain. American forces tried to invade Canada, but were unsuccessful. In retaliation, British troops briefly took Washington, D.C.

 THE NEW YORK CONNECTION

Much of the fighting in the war took place in the Great Lakes and upstate New York. The British attacked New York communities such as Sackets Harbor on Lake Ontario and Ogdensburg on the St. Lawrence River. In 1813, British troops retaliated for the attack on Canada by burning the settlement at Buffalo. Americans won a major battle of the war at Plattsburg.

In December 1814, a peace treaty was signed that left things much as they had been before the war. In the treaty, the British promised they would no longer search U.S. ships for British deserters. Thus Americans had proved they could protect their independence. The most important result of the war was a rise of American nationalism and a desire to expand the nation westwards.

National Archives

Oliver Perry at the Battle of Lake Erie

THE AGE OF JACKSON

One of the heroes of the War of 1812 was General **Andrew Jackson,** who defeated British forces at the **Battle of New Orleans** in 1815 (*before news of the peace arrived*). Jackson was elected President in 1828. A native of Tennessee, he was the first President not born to wealth and not from an Eastern state. His supporters were ordinary people, mostly laborers, farmers, and frontiersmen.

AN AGE OF REFORM

Jackson's two terms in office (1829–1836) saw an expansion of American democracy.

General Andrew Jackson

The Hermitage

DEMOCRATIC CHANGES UNDER JACKSON		
Voting Rights. After Jackson's election, states eliminated the requirement that voters own property, so that most white males over 21 could vote.	**Choosing a President.** Selection of Presidential candidates by party leaders was replaced by nominating conventions, where popularly elected members of each political party chose their candidates.	**Campaign Methods.** With increased numbers of voters, new campaign methods emerged. Candidates held dinners, rallies, and public meetings. Jackson invited ordinary people to his inauguration.

THE SPOILS SYSTEM

Jackson believed the President should act as the voice of the ordinary citizens. To make government more open to popular needs, Jackson used the **spoils system** — supporters who helped in his election campaign were appointed to government posts in place of existing officials.

JACKSON AND THE NATIVE AMERICAN INDIANS

Under Jackson's influence, Congress removed all Native American Indian settlements from lands east of the Mississippi. Among other tribes, the **Cherokees** were removed from their tribal homelands. When the Supreme Court ordered a halt to the removal, Jackson refused to enforce it. Thousands of Cherokees died along the **Trail of Tears,** when they were forcibly removed.

JACKSON AND THE FEDERAL UNION

In 1832, South Carolina threatened to secede because it opposed federal tariffs on imports. Jackson threatened force, and South Carolina backed down. Jackson emerged as a symbol of national unity over sectional interests.

A PORTRAIT OF AMERICAN SOCIETY

By the early 1800s, Americans were creating their own unique culture. It was an exciting mixture of English, European, Native American Indian, and African traditions, blended together under American conditions with democratic ideals.

FARMERS

America was overwhelmingly a rural society. Crops were the basis of the nation's wealth. Some crops, like cotton and tobacco in the South, were grown for export. Other farmers grew wheat or raised livestock to support the growing population. Owning and working the land according to the seasons of the year gave most farmers their freedom and independence.

THE RISE OF INDUSTRY

In the early 1800s, a new industrial society began to emerge in the Northeast. In the 1790s, an English worker, **Samuel Slater,** had defied British law by building from memory a machine in the U.S. that made cotton fibers into thread Slater's spinning mill was followed by a gradual increase in the use of machines, the use of steam

Library of Congress

Samuel Slater's cotton mill, near Pawtucket, Rhode Island

power, and a shift from working at home or in small shops to working in factories. These developments, known as the **Industrial Revolution,** led to new industries, expanded transportation, and rapidly growing cities. Workers in early industries often had to put in 16-hour days in factories that were crowded, poorly lit, and unsafe.

THE NEW YORK CONNECTION

In the early 1800s, it was easier and cheaper to ship goods by water than by land. In 1816, Governor **DeWitt Clinton** proposed a 360-mile canal through the Mohawk Valley, connecting Lake Erie to the Hudson River. Farmers could then ship goods from the Great Lakes to New York City entirely by water. Thousands of workers, many of them Irish immigrants, used hand tools to build the canal. Taking seven years to build, the **Erie Canal** was completed in 1825. As a

result of the Erie Canal, cities alongside its route, such as Buffalo, Rochester, Syracuse, Rome, Utica, and Albany — grew and prospered. New York City emerged as the nation's largest city.

Pulling a boat along the Erie Canal

New York's transportation system also went through other important changes. As more people moved to western New York, private companies opened special roads called **turnpikes.** The steamboat, invented by **Robert Fulton** in 1807, revolutionized water transportation. Fulton used the steam engine to drive a large wheel with paddles. Steam power was more dependable than wind, and could be used to move upstream. The railroad had a similar impact on land transportation. By 1840, railroads criss-crossed the state. The most important, the New York Central, ran through the Mohawk Valley, like the Erie Canal.

Robert Fulton

WOMEN AND FAMILY ROLES

In the early American Republic, women were usually excluded from public life and left in charge of the home and children. Men held final authority, both in household decisions and in public life.

Women were denied equality of citizenship and lacked the right to vote or to hold public office. Farm women worked in the fields and cooked, cleaned, made clothes, and cared for their children. Many women worked outside the home as servants, laundresses, cooks, and factory workers. Children were expected to respect and obey their parents. Often they worked on the farm, in addition to helping with household chores. Most had limited, if any schooling.

Women often worked the farm land

THE NEW YORK CONNECTION

Elizabeth Cady Stanton, Lucretia Mott, and others organized the **Seneca Falls Convention** in New York in 1848. The convention passed a declaration similar to the Declaration of Independence. It called for women to receive equal rights with men. The declaration helped launch a movement to change women's role in society. This movement later led to the passage of the Nineteenth Amendment (1920) — giving women the right to vote.

Lucretia Mott

AFRICAN AMERICANS

Since the 1500s, Africans had been brought to the Americas as slaves. However, in 1808, Congress prohibited the future importation of slaves. Despite America's democratic ideals, slavery continued. After 1808, most American slaves were native-born. Generally, African Americans fell into two groups:

★ **Free African Americans.** Many slaves were set free following the American Revolution. Others were freed when their owners died. Freedmen worked in a variety of occupations. However, most still faced prejudice. Laws kept them from voting, traveling, and serving on juries. Lastly, many free African Americans feared being kidnapped and returned to a life of slavery.

★ **Slaves.** Even in Southern slave-holding states, most white families had no slaves. Slaves generally were owned by wealthy Southern landholders who grew cash crops such as tobacco, cotton, and sugar. The slaves endured back-breaking work on plantations as field hands. Living conditions were usually primitive. Enslaved workers ate simple, unbalanced meals of corn, pork, and molasses.

Not all slaves worked on plantations or for the wealthy. Some slaves became skilled blacksmiths or carpenters and were hired out by their owners. Even then, their wages remained the property of their owners. Enslaved African Americans were denied basic human rights: for example, they could be sold apart from their families at the whim of their owners. Despite these harsh conditions, African Americans held onto much of their African heritage and developed their own unique culture.

A Slave Auction

Library of Congress

THE NEW YORK CONNECTION

By 1820, New York was the most populous state in the country. New York also became an important center for reform. Abolitionists opposed slavery, which became illegal in New York State in 1827. **Dorothea Dix** fought for the rights of the mentally ill. The state legislature passed laws providing money for public education, and New York became a leader in the number and quality of its schools. All students became entitled to a free elementary school education.

Erasmus Hall Academy, now Erasmus H.S., is one of the oldest schools in the state

New York State Archives

SUMMARIZING YOUR UNDERSTANDING

OVERARCHING THEME

*The final source of political power
in our system of government is the people.*

KEY TERMS, CONCEPTS, AND PEOPLE

★ Articles of Confederation

★ Northwest Ordinance, 1787

★ U.S. Constitution

★ "Great Compromise"

★ Bill of Rights

★ Hamilton's Financial Plan

★ Political Parties

★ Louisiana Purchase

★ War of 1812

★ Jacksonian Democracy

TESTING YOUR UNDERSTANDING

MULTIPLE-CHOICE QUESTIONS

1 **The greatest problem facing the newly independent states was**
  1 attracting foreign nations to build factories in America
  2 bringing about lower taxes
  3 creating some type of a central government
  4 establishing a Supreme Court

2 **One weakness of the Articles of Confederation was that it**
  1 gave too little power to the national government
  2 rejected the idea of a democratic government
  3 established a national court system
  4 created too many political parties

3   At the Constitutional Convention of 1787, the agreement known as the "Great Compromise" concerned

  1   each state's representation in Congress
  2   the powers of the President
  3   how to count slaves for representation in Congress
  4   foreign trade

4   In our system of democracy, final political power rests with the

  1   U.S. Supreme Court   3   President of the United States
  2   U.S. Congress   4   people of the nation

Base your answer to questions 5 on the table below.

RATIFICATION OF THE U.S. CONSTITUTION

STATE	DATE	STATE	DATE	STATE	DATE
Delaware	1787	Massachusetts	1788	Virginia	1788
Pennsylvania	1787	Maryland	1788	New York	1788
New Jersey	1787	South Carolina	1788	North Carolina	1788
Georgia	1788	New Hampshire	1788	Rhode Island	1790
Connecticut	1788				

5   In what year did most states ratify the U.S. Constitution?

  1   1787   3   1789
  2   1788   4   1790

6   The purpose of the checks and balances in the Constitution is to

  1   explain the President's treaty-making powers
  2   prevent any one branch of government from becoming too powerful
  3   list the procedures for introducing bills into Congress
  4   allow each branch of government to veto laws it objects to

7   The authors of the Constitution believed that

  1   the President should impeach corrupt government officials
  2   a government should have limited powers
  3   the President should have control over Congress
  4   slaves and women should have the right to vote

8   The first ten amendments to the Constitution were added to

    1   provide a strong judiciary   **3**   assure citizens of fair elections

    2   protect the rights of individuals   **4**   maintain a powerful army

Base your answers to question 9 on the diagram below.

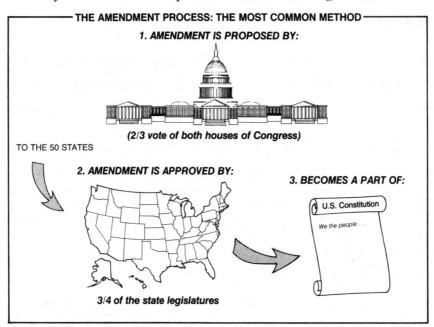

9   Why did the authors of the Constitution make the amendment process so difficult?

    1   to prevent changes except by widespread agreement

    2   to prevent the government from becoming undemocratic

    3   to allow the U.S. Constitution to keep pace with changing times

    4   to make it the same process as passing a law

10   Repaying the national debt, creating a national bank, and passing a whiskey tax were economic policies favored by

    1   Thomas Jefferson   **3**   Benjamin Franklin

    2   Alexander Hamilton   **4**   Andrew Jackson

11   Which statement best summarizes the views of Thomas Jefferson?

    1   Only the wealthy should be allowed to serve in government.

    2   The nation needs a powerful central government if it is to survive.

    3   Government is best when it governs least.

    4   The United States needs a large military.

12 The American Revolution and the War of 1812 were similar in that both

    1   led to the principle of "no taxation without representation"

    2   helped lead to the downfall of the Federalist Party

    3   were fought against the British

    4   represented defeats for the United States

13 A supporter of Jacksonian democracy would favor the idea of

    1   government in the hands of an elected king or queen

    2   a President selected by political party leaders

    3   government service equally open to all individuals

    4   reduced military spending

14 In an outline, one of these is the main topic. The others are sub-topics. Which is the main topic?

    1   Building of the Erie Canal

    2   Opening of Turnpikes

    3   Invention of the Steamboat

    4   Transportation Revolution

CONSTRUCTED-RESPONSE QUESTIONS

Base your answers to questions 1 through 3 on the table below.

Some Provisions of the Articles of Confederation
• One vote for each state, regardless of its size.
• Congress was powerless to impose and collect taxes.
• No separate executive to enforce acts of Congress.
• Amendments only with the agreement of all the states.
• Agreement of 9 states required to pass a law.

1. How many states were needed in order to pass a law? _____

2. What were the Articles of Confederation? _____

_____

3. State **one** argument made by opponents of the Articles of Confederation. _____

_____

Base your answers to questions 4 through 6 on the passage below.

*W*e hold these truths to be self-evident: that all men and women are created equal; that they are endowed by their Creator (**God**) with certain unalienable (**basic**) rights. The history of mankind is a history of repeated injuries on the part of man toward woman, having as its direct object (**purpose**) the establishment of an absolute tyranny (**total power**) over her. To prove this, let the facts be given to the world: He has never permitted her to exercise her unalienable right to vote. He has forced her to submit (**give in**) to laws she had no voice in forming. He has taken from her all right to property, even the wages she earns.

— *Adopted by the Seneca Falls Convention, 1848*

4. Which convention adopted this declaration? _____

5. Identify the document from which this declaration was modeled. _____

_____

6. Identify **one** reformer who helped get this declaration adopted. _____

_____

7. What impact did this declaration have on the Women's Rights Movement?

_____

DOCUMENT-BASED QUESTIONS: UNDERSTANDING THE "ACTION WORDS"

The document-based essay question on the **Grade 8 Intermediate Social Studies Test** will require you to understand certain key words. The instructions telling you what you are supposed to do in writing your answer are contained in the "action words." The most common "action words" are:

Describe or Discuss

Explain or Show How

Evaluate

In this section we will examine each of these "action words" to see specifically what they require you to do in answering a document-based essay question.

DESCRIBE OR DISCUSS

Describe or *discuss* means to "illustrate something in words or to tell about it." "Describe" or "discuss" is used when you are asked for the **who, what, when,** and **where** of something. Not every "describe" or "discuss" question requires all four of these elements. However, your answer must go beyond just a single word or sentence. The following are examples that show how "describe" and "discuss" may be used in a document-based essay question:

> ★ *Describe* an achievement of the Seneca Falls Convention.
>
> ★ *Discuss* the differences in views of Alexander Hamilton and Thomas Jefferson on the role of government.

EXPLAIN AND SHOW

The words *explain* and *show* are often linked to the additional word *how* or *why.* The key in approaching a question with these words is to determine whether the question requires you to give an answer for *how* something happened or *why* it happened.

EXPLAIN HOW QUESTIONS

This type of question asks you to explain "how" something works or "how" it relates to something else. "How" means *in what way.* These questions usually focus on events or effects, not causes. Let's look at two examples:

> ★ *Show how* Washington's Presidency had a lasting impact on the nation.
>
> ★ *Explain how* changes under President Jackson affected the coutry's political development.

In each case you are expected to provide facts and examples that show *how* the generalization is true. In these examples, you would present the effects of Washington's Presidency and of Jacksonian democracy.

WHY QUESTIONS

To explain *why* means to give reasons why an event took place or why a relationship identified in the question occurred. *Explain why* questions focus on causes. Your answer should identify the reasons why the event or relationship took place and briefly describe each reason. Two examples of such questions are:

★ *Show why* Americans decided to write a new constitution in 1787.

★ *Explain why* the United States declared war on Great Britain in 1812.

In each case, you must present reasons or causes to explain *why* the event occurred.

EVALUATE

Evaluate means "to examine and judge carefully." *Evaluate* questions ask you to make a judgment. In answering such a question, you must consider the advantages and disadvantages of the policy or action you are evaluating. Then decide whether the advantages outweigh the disadvantages or the reverse. Let's look at a typical evaluate question:

Evaluate the positive and negative effects of the early Industrial Revolution on the United States.

In order to properly answer this question, here is what you must do:

★ *Explain* what the early Industrial Revolution was.

★ *Identify* both the positive (*good*) and negative (*bad*) effects of the early Industrial Revolution on the United States.

★ *Make a judgment* about whether the overall impact was either positive or negative.

CHAPTER 7

THE UNION TESTED,
From 1840 to 1877

In this chapter, you will learn how the new nation expanded its borders to the Pacific coast. The nation also endured its first great test since independence — the Civil War. After five years of fighting, the Union was preserved and slavery came to an end. During the Reconstruction era, Southerners endured military occupation by the North. As you read this chapter, you will learn about:

Charleston, South Carolina (1865) — the south lay in ruins after the Civil War

Library of Congress

★ **The United States Expands.** Soon after independence, Americans set a course for Westward expansion. The expansion of the United States posed new challenges, as Americans debated whether new territories should enter the union as slave states or free states.

★ **The Civil War.** When Lincoln was elected President, Southern states seceded. The North's larger population, manufacturing facilities and naval power enabled it to win the war and end slavery.

★ **The Reconstruction Era.** Congress imposed military rule and Reconstruction governments on the South. Following Reconstruction, Southern states introduced racial segregation and denied African Americans many hard-won rights.

In studying this period, you should focus on the following questions:

★ How did the nation establish its present borders?

★ What were the main causes of the Civil War?

★ What problems arose during the Reconstruction Era?

★ How was New York affected by the Civil War?

MAJOR THEMES IN U.S. HISTORY: TURNING POINTS

WHAT IS A TURNING POINT?

Certain times in our lives are more important than others. When we first learn to talk and our first day of school are important turning points in our lives. A **turning point** is a moment of change — when we move from one stage of life to a new and different stage.

A society also reaches times of major change, or turning points. This often happens when a country goes to war, faces an economic crisis, or experiences a major change in government. Choices by leaders at such critical turning points can be especially decisive.

National Archives

The Civil War was one of the major turning points in this nation's history

Some turning points affect the entire development and direction of a society. For example, President Jefferson's decision to buy the Louisiana Territory in 1803 greatly influenced the development of the United States by placing it on the road to westward expansion. The Civil War, which you will read about in this chapter, was equally a turning point. It ended slavery and confirmed the supremacy of the federal government over the states.

MAJOR TURNING POINTS IN U.S. HISTORY

Historians are particularly interested in studying major turning points in history because they want to understand what forces lead to such major changes. Here are some of the key turning points in American history.

TURNING POINT	DESCRIPTION
The American Revolution (1775–1783)	On July 4, 1776, delegates representing the thirteen colonies issued the Declaration of Independence, proclaiming their independence from Great Britain. The colonies became states in a new country — the United States.
Constitutional Convention	The Constitution established a new government based on democracy, federalism, and the separation of powers.
Westward Expansion (1804–1848)	The Louisiana Purchase (1803) doubled the size of the nation. Americans later annexed California and the Southwest after the Mexican-American War (1846–1848). The United States now occupied lands from coast to coast.
The Civil War (1861–1865)	Sectionalism led to different ways of life in different parts of the nation. Lincoln's election in 1860 led the Southern states to secede. The North achieved victory after four years of warfare, ended slavery, and confirmed federal supremacy.
Reconstruction (1865–1877)	During Reconstruction, Americans had to rebuild the South and reunite with the Union. Congress refused to recognize Southern state governments and imposed military rule. Reconstruction ended in 1877. Southern state governments deprived African Americans of their recently won rights and introduced segregation.
Industrialization and settlement of the West	After the Civil War, America was transformed by industrialization, urbanization, immigration, the expansion of the railroads, and the settlement of the West. Native American Indians were forced onto reservations. The construction of railroads tied the nation together, and greater numbers of Americans moved into cities. America rapidly became an industrial and urban society.
The Progressive Era (1890–1919)	Muckrakers and other middle-class reformers exposed the abuses caused by the rise of big business and rapid industrialization. Progressive state governments and Presidents Theodore Roosevelt and Woodrow Wilson passed laws to curb some of the worst abuses.
The Roaring Twenties (1920s)	The passage of the 19th Amendment and the prosperity of the 1920s saw the rise of new cultural values. Women, African Americans and youths enjoyed greater freedom and influence than ever before.
Depression, and the New Deal, (1930s)	The New York Stock Market Crash of 1929 led to the Great Depression. President Roosevelt's "New Deal" introduced new programs to find people work. He introduced Social Security and other reforms. The federal government took responsibility for the smooth running of the nation's economy.
The Civil Rights Movement (1950s–1960s)	The *Brown v. Board of Education* decision (1954) inaugurated the Civil Rights Movement. Under Dr. King and others, African Americans ended racial segregation while making tremendous strides towards racial equality. The Civil Rights Movement was followed by the Women's Liberation Movement, in which women achieved greater equality in the workplace and at home.
The Computer Revolution (1980–2000s)	The modern computer was first developed during World War II. However, the later introduction of silicon circuit boards made smaller and more powerful computers possible. In recent decades, computerization, the Internet, and cell phones have transformed almost every aspect of American life.

MAJOR HISTORICAL DEVELOPMENTS

THE NATION EXPANDS ITS TERRITORY

In its first years after independence, the United States was relatively weak and feared more powerful European nations. As a result, President Washington felt the new nation should develop on its own rather than get entangled in developments in Europe.

AMERICA MOVES TO SECURE ITS BORDERS

As the nation began to grow and prosper, the focus of its foreign policy changed from neutrality to securing its borders from foreign threats.

LOUISIANA PURCHASE, 1803

In 1803, France offered to sell the area it controlled west of the Mississippi River. Despite doubts about its constitutionality, President Jefferson purchased the Louisiana Territory, doubling the size of the United States.

THE WAR OF 1812

In 1812, the nation went to war with Great Britain to stop the British from taking sailors off American ships. Some Americans hoped to use the war as an excuse to invade and conquer Canada. The war ended in 1814 with no clear winner.

THE CESSION OF FLORIDA, 1819

The purchase of the Louisiana Territory and the end of the War of 1812 caused many Americans to look to expand towards the west. Much of this territory, however, was still claimed by Spain. Americans negotiated the purchase of Florida, in the south, from Spain in 1819.

THE MONROE DOCTRINE, 1823

Between 1810 and 1822, most of Spain's Latin American colonies rebelled and became independent. The United States feared Spain or other European nations might try to reconquer them. In 1823, **President James Monroe** stated that the U.S. would oppose any attempt by European nations to establish new colonies in the Western Hemisphere or to reconquer former colonies. Monroe also stated, however, that the United States would not interfere with existing European colonies like Canada and Cuba.

MANIFEST DESTINY

The construction of the Erie Canal helped stimulate the settlement of the Midwest. Settlers filled the lands of the old Northwest Territory, which now became new states. Many Americans came to believe it was America's **Manifest Destiny** (*clear future*) to extend the nation to the shores of the Pacific.

★ **Annexation of Texas (1845).** An opportunity to expand the nation's borders came in 1836, when settlers in the Mexican province of Texas declared independence and defeated Mexican forces. In 1845, Congress voted to make Texas part of the United States.

★ **Oregon Territory (1846).** In an agreement with Great Britain, the line dividing Canada and the United States was extended westwards to the Pacific.

★ **Mexican-American War (1846–1848).** A dispute between the United States and Mexico over the Texas border led to the Mexican-American War. After the United States won the war, Mexico ceded territory now occupied by California, Nevada, Utah, Arizona, Colorado, and New Mexico.

★ **Alaska (1867).** The United States purchased Alaska from Russia just after the Civil War.

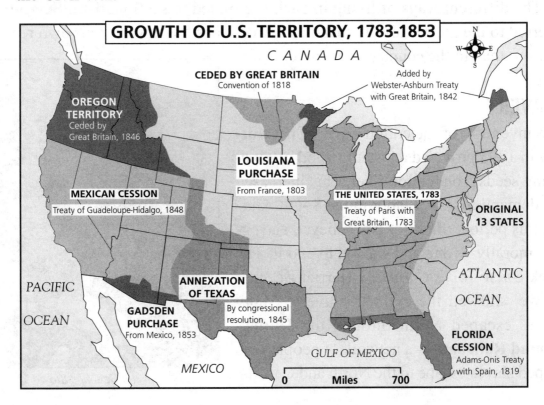

GROWTH OF U.S. TERRITORY, 1783-1853

THE CIVIL WAR, 1860–1865

The Civil War was the bloodiest war in American history. Like most wars, it had several causes.

CAUSES OF THE CIVIL WAR

SECTIONALISM

During the early 1800s, America became divided into sections. The Northern, Southern and Western sections of the United States each developed their own unique economic and cultural ways of life.

★ **North.** The North became a center of manufacturing, shipping, fishing, and small farms.

★ **South.** Most Southerners did not own slaves. However, much of their economy was based on profits from the use of slave labor on large plantations to grow crops like cotton for sale to England or the Northeast.

★ **West.** Western states (*now the "Midwest"*) became the nation's breadbasket, growing and shipping grain to the North and South.

The different ways of living in each region led to sectionalism. **Sectionalism** referred to the greater loyalty that many Americans felt toward their own region (*or section*) than to the country as a whole.

SLAVERY

The invention of the cotton gin by **Eli Whitney** in 1793 provided a faster method of separating seeds from cotton fiber. This increased the demand for slave labor in the South. During this period, **abolitionists** believed slavery was morally wrong and wanted to end it. The book *Uncle Tom's Cabin,* by Harriet Beecher Stowe, showed the evils of slavery. Many slaves escaped North through the **Underground Railroad** — a network of people who helped slaves escape to the North and Canada.

Harriet Beecher Stowe

STATES' RIGHTS

Many Southerners believed that each state had the power to reject federal law or even to leave the Union altogether if it wished.

WESTERN EXPANSION

As the nation expanded westward, new states were added. This posed the problem of whether these new states should enter the Union as slave or free states.

THE BREAKDOWN OF COMPROMISE

To keep the Union together, the states agreed to a series of compromises from 1820 onwards. The **Missouri Compromise of 1820** and the **Compromise of 1850** were able to temporarily keep the peace. However, in the 1850s these earlier compromises broke down, making a conflict between the North and South almost inevitable.

★ **Kansas-Nebraska Act.** In 1854, Congress passed a law allowing settlers in these two states to decide for themselves whether or not they wanted slavery. This resulted in bloodshed between those who favored and those who opposed slavery.

★ **Dred Scott Decision.** In 1857, the Supreme Court ruled that Congress could not prohibit slavery in any new territories. Even though Dred Scott had lived in a free territory, the court ruled he was still a slave without rights. The Court argued that slaves were property and that Congress had no right to take away a slaveholder's property.

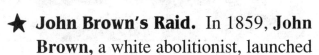

Dred Scott

Schomburg Center for Black Culture

★ **John Brown's Raid.** In 1859, **John Brown,** a white abolitionist, launched a slave revolt. His uprising was quickly crushed, and he was tried and executed. Brown's attempted uprising rang an alarm bell among Southerners, who feared future slave revolts.

U.S. During the Civil War, 1861–1865

HIGHLIGHTS OF THE CIVIL WAR
===

The **Republican Party** was formed in 1854 to oppose the spread of slavery to new territories. In 1860, Republican candidate **Abraham Lincoln** was elected President.

★ **Fort Sumter Attacked.** Southern states, fearing Lincoln would abolish slavery, seceded and formed the **Confederate States of America.** Lincoln acted to preserve the nation's unity. In 1861, Confederate forces attacked Fort Sumter in South Carolina. The Civil War now began.

Fort Sumter, S.C. April 4, 1861 under the Confederate flag

★ **Fighting During the Civil War.** Although the South enjoyed superior military leadership and the commitment of many Southerners to preserve their way of life, it lacked manufacturing centers or a strong navy. The North eventually triumphed because of its larger population, better transportation system, superior industry, and greater naval power.

★ **Emancipation Proclamation.** Lincoln freed the slaves in the Confederacy during the war with the Emancipation Proclamation (1862). The **Thirteenth Amendment** (1865) later abolished slavery throughout the United States.

THE NEW YORK CONNECTION

In 1863, the U.S. government passed a "draft" law requiring men to serve in the army. The draft law was unpopular with many New Yorkers. In July 1863, **draft riots** broke out in New York City protesting the law. Angry mobs attacked abolitionists and an African-American children's orphanage in New York City. The rioters believed these groups had made the draft necessary. Despite the draft riots, New Yorkers played an important role in defeating the South. Of all the states, New York sent the largest number of soldiers — almost half a million men — to fight in the Civil War.

Anti-draft rioters attack the Colored Orphans Asylum in New York City

Library of Congress

THE RECONSTRUCTION ERA

The South finally surrendered in 1865. The Civil War preserved the Union and abolished slavery. The **Reconstruction Period** (1865–1877) refers to the decade after the Civil War. At the war's end the South was in ruins — cities, railroad lines, and plantations had been destroyed by Union armies. Plantations no longer had slaves, and the freed slaves, known as **freedmen,** lacked jobs, land, and income. One additional problem facing the national government was to decide upon the conditions under which the Southern States could be admitted back into the Union.

THE BATTLE OVER RECONSTRUCTION PLANS

Lincoln had planned to readmit Southern states to the Union on lenient terms, but was assassinated in 1865. The **Radical Republicans** in Congress refused to recognize new Southern state governments. Instead, they imposed military rule and passed a **Civil Rights Act** giving freedmen full rights. This act became the basis for the later **Fourteenth Amendment,** which declared that no state government could deny American citizens full rights or equality before the law. **Andrew Johnson** became President after Lincoln's assassination. When Johnson opposed the Congressional reconstruction plan, Radical Republicans in Congress moved to **impeach** him. During Johnson's impeachment trial, the Senate failed — by only one vote — to remove him from office.

President Andrew Johnson

Library of Congress

THE RECONSTRUCTION GOVERNMENTS

During the Reconstruction period, former Confederates were barred from voting or holding office. Instead, freedmen and so-called **carpetbaggers** (*people from the north*) and **scalawags** (*white Southerners who opposed the Confederacy*) held power.

Reconstruction governments built new schools, roads and railroads, and banned racial discrimination. To deal with economic problems, plantation owners and freedmen developed the system of **sharecropping.** Former plantation owners provided livestock, tools, and land to former slaves in exchange for a share of their crop.

The first African Americans to serve in the House of Representatives during Reconstruction

Library of Congress

RECONSTRUCTION ENDS

Reconstruction ended when Northern troops withdrew in 1877. Former Confederate leaders returned to power, and freedmen lost most of their newly achieved rights. The **Ku Klux Klan** terrorized Southern blacks who challenged white control. Southern state governments passed **Jim Crow laws**, segregating whites from blacks in schools and other public facilities. These "separate but equal" laws were upheld by the Supreme Court in *Plessy v. Ferguson* (1896). In the late 19th and early 20th centuries, African-American leaders such as **Booker T. Washington,** author of the book *Up From Slavery,* and **W.E.B. DuBois,** founder of the N.A.A.C.P., spoke out against these injustices.

W.E.B. DuBois

Library of Congress

THE NEW YORK CONNECTION

Women New Yorkers played a key role during the Civil War and after. New Yorker **Dr. Mary E. Walker** achieved fame as a surgeon with the Union Army. **Dr. Elizabeth Blackwell,** the first female doctor in the nation, was a leader of the U.S. Sanitary Commission. **Harriet Tubman,** an abolitionist, led some 300 hundred runaway slaves to freedom. The economic effects following the war caused divisions among New Yorkers. Some made money from selling war materials. But for most New Yorkers, the cost of living had greatly increased. The growing gap between rich and poor New Yorkers led to hard feelings. On the positive side, New York emerged as the leading industrial state of the nation.

Mary Walker on her wedding day

Library of Congress

SUMMARIZING YOUR UNDERSTANDING

OVERARCHING THEME

The Civil War settled the issue of slavery and saved the Union, but left many new issues unresolved.

KEY TERMS, CONCEPTS, AND PEOPLE

★ Monroe Doctrine

★ Manifest Destiny

★ Abolitionist

★ Dred Scott Decision

★ Civil War

★ Abraham Lincoln

★ Emancipation Proclamation

★ Reconstruction Era

TESTING YOUR UNDERSTANDING

MULTIPLE-CHOICE QUESTIONS

1   A major reason for issuing the Monroe Doctrine was to
   1   halt the slave trade from Africa to the United States
   2   prevent European involvement in the Western Hemisphere
   3   keep the United States from going to war with Mexico
   4   protect American sailors on the high seas

2   Which term best identifies the desire of many Americans to expand westward in the 1800s?
   1   neutrality
   2   imperialism
   3   Manifest Destiny
   4   sectionalism

3 **The Louisiana Purchase, the annexation of Texas, and the Mexican-American War had in common the fact that they resulted in**

   1 war between the Union States and Spain

   2 giving land to the Native American Indians

   3 additional territory for the United States

   4 opening the Caribbean area to American investment

Base your answers to questions 4 and 5 on the graph below.

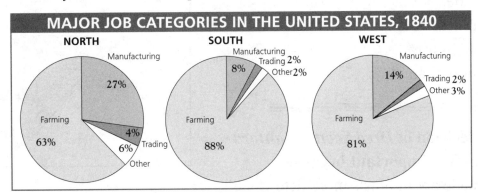

4 **At which job did most Americans work in 1840?**

   1 farming   **3** trading

   2 manufacturing   **4** shipping

5 **Based on the graph, which statement is most accurate?**

   1 Manufacturing was the major occupation in the South.

   2 In the North, most people were employed in trading.

   3 Occupations such as shipping and craftsmanship dominated the South.

   4 A larger percentage of people worked in manufacturing in the North than in the South or West.

6 **"Compromise Enables Maine and Missouri to Enter Union"**
"California Admitted to Union as a Free State"
"Kansas-Nebraska Act Establishes Popular Sovereignty"
Which public issue is reflected in these headlines?

   1 enactment of tariffs   **3** the extension of slavery

   2 voting rights for minorities   **4** free public education

7 **An "abolitionist" was a person who**

   1 believed in free trade   **3** wanted to end slavery

   2 opposed foreign alliances   **4** supported obtaining colonies

8   A major cause of the Civil War was

  1   the secession of Southern states   3   freedom of the seas

  2   the annexation of Texas   4   the right of women to vote

Base your answers to question 9 on the graph below.

9   What percentage of Southern families did not own slaves?

  1   under 50%

  2   almost 70%

  3   about 60%

  4   more than 80%

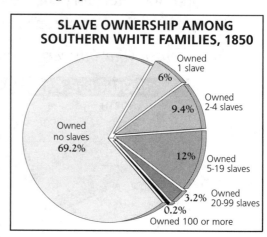

SLAVE OWNERSHIP AMONG SOUTHERN WHITE FAMILIES, 1850

Owned 1 slave 6%
Owned 2-4 slaves 9.4%
Owned no slaves 69.2%
Owned 5-19 slaves 12%
Owned 20-99 slaves 3.2%
Owned 100 or more 0.2%

10   The decision of *Dred Scott v. Sanford* (1857) was important because it

  1   made abolitionists more determined to achieve their goals

  2   resulted in the immediate outbreak of the Civil War

  3   ended the importation of slaves into the United States

  4   increased Congressional power to ban slavery from new territories

11   Which best describes why President Lincoln went to war against the South during the Civil War?

  1   Lincoln strongly desired to end slavery.

  2   Lincoln wanted to keep the South dependent on the North.

  3   Lincoln was determined to preserve the Union.

  4   Lincoln wanted to protect freedom of the seas.

12   The purpose of the Emancipation Proclamation was to

  1   return slaves to Africa   3   free slaves in the Confederacy

  2   support states' rights   4   create new state governments

13   Racial segregation in the South after Reconstruction was based on the belief that

  1   each culture has contributed equally to American society

  2   some racial groups are superior to others

  3   people should be treated equally regardless of race

  4   the freedmen required special assistance

14 **Scalawags, sharecropping, and Radical Republicans are terms most closely identified with which time period in American history?**
  1 American Revolution
  3 Civil War
  2 War of 1812
  4 Reconstruction Era

15 **The decision of the U.S. Supreme Court in *Plessy v. Ferguson***
  1 outlawed segregation
  2 allowed slavery in new territories
  3 legalized segregation
  4 banned slavery in new territories

CONSTRUCTED-RESPONSE QUESTION

Base your answers to questions 1 through 3 on the table below.

RESOURCES OF THE NORTH AND SOUTH, 1861
(Expressed as Percentages)

RESOURCE	North	South
Total Population	71%	29%
Factories	85%	15%
Farmland	65%	35%
Railroad Miles	71%	29%
Bank Deposits	78%	22%

Source: *Historical Statistics of the United States*

1. What is the source of this chart? _____

2. What percentage of the nation's total bank deposits were held by Southern banks?

3. With which war in American history would the figures in this table be associated?

4. What does this table show about the resources of the North and South in 1861?

DOCUMENT-BASED QUESTIONS: LEARNING TO WRITE GOOD PARAGRAPHS

Because of the importance of good writing in a well-organized document-based essay, this section looks more closely at the process of writing a good paragraph. A **paragraph** is a group of sentences that deals with the same *topic* or *theme*. A good paragraph displays three important characteristics:

1 Unity   2 Completeness   3 Order

UNITY

Every paragraph should be unified — all the sentences in the paragraph should deal with a single topic. Sentences not related to the topic of the paragraph should be moved to other paragraphs. Writers often use a topic sentence to give a paragraph unity. **Topic sentences** identify, in a single sentence, the main idea of each paragraph. All sentences in the paragraph should be related to the topic sentence. Let's see how this might appear:

Topic Sentence

> *One of the most important causes of the Civil War was the issue of slavery. Slavery was important to the South's economy. Plantation owners used slaves to grow cotton and other crops. Southerners did not think slavery was wrong. They pointed to slavery in the Bible and in other societies. Slave owners also felt their slaves were better treated than many Northern factory workers. In the North, the economy was based on free laborers. Most Northerners believed the nation could not continue half-slave and half-free. Eventually, these conflicting attitudes over slavery led to the Civil War.*

Notice how several sentences in this paragraph specifically use the word "slavery." This helps to tie the entire paragraph together for the reader.

COMPLETENESS

A second characteristic of a good paragraph is completeness. Each paragraph should thoroughly develop the idea expressed in its topic sentence.

In general, you should provide enough details and supporting facts that, after reading your paragraph, your reader:

 will understand the main idea of your topic sentence,

and

 will have enough details to conclude that your main idea is correct.

To see if your idea is complete, pretend you are the reader and re-read the paragraph. Does it meet the above criteria for completeness? Do you have to add further information to make your point?

How long should a paragraph be? Again, the answer depends. If there is not enough information in the paragraph to support the main idea, then the paragraph is too short. If the paragraph is very long, it may deal with many aspects of the same topic and should be broken up. Following is a paragraph with a topic sentence and details to support it:

Topic Sentence

> Many reasons explain the Union victory over the Confederacy. The North had 22 million people, while the South had only 9 million. Nearly 4 million of these Southerners were slaves. Fearing a rebellion, the Southerners were unwilling to put weapons in the hands of their slaves. In addition, over 90 percent of the nation's factories were in the North. The North had twice as many miles of railroad track as the South. This advantage allowed the North to easily move and supply its armies in the field. Finally, Lincoln used the North's superior navy to set up a blockade. Southerners could not ship their cotton to England or get help.

Do you think this paragraph is complete? Do the details show the many reasons explaining the Union victory over the Confederacy?

ORDER

All the sentences of the paragraph should be presented in a logical order. This is one of the most essential parts of writing. The direction in which the paragraph moves depends on the purpose of the paragraph. Here are some of the most common ways for logically presenting information in a paragraph:

★ **Sequential (Chronology).** This paragraph presents a series of events or steps in the order in which they occurred.

★ **From the General to the Specific.** This paragraph opens with a general topic sentence and then provides examples to explain it. The examples could be organized from the most important to the least, or from the least important to the most.

★ **From the Specific to the General.** A paragraph may also start with a series of examples or details that lead to a more general conclusion. The conclusion at the end of the paragraph can serve as the topic sentence.

★ **Parts to a Whole.** Here, the purpose of the paragraph is to describe a number of "parts" to something. The parts should be described in any order that makes sense to the reader. If describing a scene, you might describe the scene moving from right to left, or from the least to most important.

★ **Cause and Effect.** Another way to organize a paragraph is to begin with an effect, stated in the topic sentence, followed by its causes. For example, the topic sentence could be stated either as a question, such as "Why did Americans go to war in 1812?" or as a statement: "There were many reasons why Americans went to war in 1812." The rest of the paragraph would then list the causes of U.S. involvement in the war.

Good writers also rely on transition words to help make one of these orders more obvious. **Transition words** let a reader know what to expect.

FUNCTION	TRANSITIONAL PHRASE
To explain a new point about the topic	*Moreover, in addition, also, furthermore, then, similarly, again, next, secondly, finally*
To introduce an example	*For example, thus, to illustrate, in this case*
To introduce a conclusion or effect	*Therefore, in conclusion, thus, to sum up, as a result, in consequence*
To mention a contrast or qualification	*Nevertheless, on the other hand, nonetheless, however, despite*

CHAPTER 8

THE INDUSTRIALIZATION OF AMERICA,
From 1877 to 1918

In this chapter, you will learn how the United States became one of the world's leading industrial powers after the Civil War. Industrialization touched almost every aspect of life in America. It meant new products and conveniences for consumers and new sources of wealth for business-owners. It is helpful to think of these changes as occurring in the following areas:

Immigrants poured into the United States from Europe in ever-increasing numbers

Library of Congress

★ **Rise of American Industry.** The development of new machines led to the rise of factories and mass production. Often ill-treated by their employers, factory workers organized into unions. At first, public opinion opposed unions, but attitudes changed in the early 1900s.

★ **Immigration and Urbanization.** People flooded into cities in search of jobs and prosperity. Immigrants were attracted by dreams of a better life. Cities grew so rapidly they could not deal with their problems.

★ **Settlement of the Frontier.** Wilderness areas began to disappear as settlers and farmers moved West. Native American Indians were forced off their traditional lands and moved onto government reservations.

In studying this period, you should focus on the following questions:

★ What factors led to the emergence of the U.S. as an industrial giant?

★ How were workers affected by the rise of industry?

★ What factors led to increasing immigration to the United States?

★ How were Native American Indians affected by the movement west?

MAJOR THEMES IN U.S. HISTORY: ECONOMICS

The **Industrial Revolution** began in England in the 1750s. It set in motion a period of growth and change unique in human history. To understand the Industrial Revolution and its influence on American life, let's look briefly at what an economy is, how a free market economy works, and the causes and effects of economic change.

HOW SOCIETIES MEET THEIR ECONOMIC NEEDS

We all have wants and needs. Unfortunately, our wants are unlimited and can never be fully satisfied because we have limited resources. A society can never meet everyone's wants and needs with its existing resources. This is the **problem of scarcity.** Because of the problem of scarcity, every society must make choices in answering three basic economic questions:

1 What should be produced?	2 How should it be produced?	3 Who gets what is produced?

Economics is the study of how societies use their limited resources to satisfy these unlimited wants. Societies answer these basic economic questions in three ways. Each way is referred to as an **economic system.**

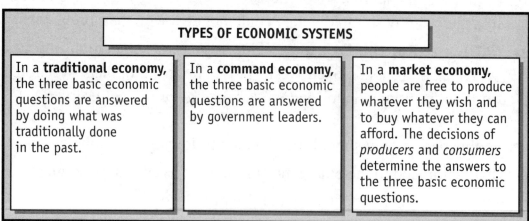

TYPES OF ECONOMIC SYSTEMS		
In a **traditional economy,** the three basic economic questions are answered by doing what was traditionally done in the past.	In a **command economy,** the three basic economic questions are answered by government leaders.	In a **market economy,** people are free to produce whatever they wish and to buy whatever they can afford. The decisions of *producers* and *consumers* determine the answers to the three basic economic questions.

A **producer** is someone who provides a good or service. A **consumer** is someone who purchases or uses a good or service.

THE FACTORS OF PRODUCTION

In order to provide goods and services, producers make use of the resources of a society. These include natural, human, and capital resources.

★ **Natural Resources** are the minerals, plants, and animals found in nature — including air, water, and soil. These allow us to grow crops or provide the materials and energy needed to make goods.

★ **Human Resources** are the human labor and management skills that go into making goods and providing services.

★ **Capital Resources** are the results of reshaping natural and human resources into tools that

What are some of the factors of production that went into making this home?

aid in the making of future goods and services. Factories, canals, ships and railroads are examples of capital resources. Money is also a capital resource.

HOW THE FREE MARKET WORKS

In a free market economy, the **profit motive** provides an incentive for people to risk their money to produce goods and to provide services. The forces of supply and demand help set the price for a product and determine how much is made. **Supply** refers to how much of a product producers make. **Demand** is how much of a product consumers are willing to buy.

★ When demand is high and supply is low, the price goes up.

★ When demand is low and supply is high, the price goes down.

Producers who charge too much for a good or service lose customers to those who can produce items more efficiently and charge less.

MAJOR HISTORICAL DEVELOPMENTS

THE RISE OF AMERICAN INDUSTRY

Two hundred years ago, most people lived on farms and made goods by hand. During the **Industrial Revolution,** people began producing goods in factories using machines driven by steam power. In the period following the Civil War, the United States emerged as one of the world's leading industrialized nations. A major factor in the industrialization of the nation was its economic system — **capitalism,** sometimes called the **free market** or **free enterprise system.** Under capitalism, wealth is privately owned rather than controlled by government. Investors risk their money in businesses in the hope of making a profit. Consumers are free to choose what they wish to buy.

STEPS ON THE ROAD TO BECOMING AN INDUSTRIAL GIANT

There are several reasons that help to explain the nation's rise as an industrial giant.

THE GROWTH OF THE RAILROADS

One key to the growth of the United States as an industrial power was the building of railroads. In 1869, the first **transcontinental railroad,** connecting the East and West Coasts of the nation, was completed. Soon other railroad lines were built. Railroads brought people from the East to the western frontier. They made it possible to move food from farms and goods from factories to distant cities. Railroad advertisements describing new opportunities attracted many immigrants to the United States.

Completion of the transcontinental railroad at Promontory Point, Utah

Library of Congress

NEW INVENTIONS AND WAYS OF PRODUCING GOODS

New technologies helped fuel the economic expansion of the late 1800s. The Bessemer process, developed in the 1850s, made the production of steel more economical. In 1859, the first oil well was drilled in Pennsylvania. In 1844, **Samuel F.B. Morse's** invention of the telegraph signaled the start of a revolution in communications. **Alexander Graham Bell** invented the telephone (1876). After experimenting with an electric current to transmit sounds, **Thomas A. Edison** developed the electric light bulb (1879). By 1900, electricity was used to power motors, electric street cars, and subways.

Library of Congress

Alexander Graham Bell

THE RISE OF CORPORATIONS

Before the Civil War, most businesses were owned by individuals or partners. After the Civil War, the **corporation** became a very popular form of business. A key advantage of a corporation is that it can raise extremely large sums of money by selling **stocks** (*shares of the business*) to anyone who wishes to buy them.

People who purchase shares in a corporation are called **stockholders.** Each stockholder is a part owner of the corporation and shares in corporate profits.

Corporations used the money they raised to build large machines and factories. This enabled them to produce goods more cheaply.

As a result of these factors, the number and size of businesses in America began to expand rapidly in the years following the Civil War. The number and skill of workers also increased.

Jarrett Archives

*A 100-share stock certificate from
John D. Rockefeller's Standard Oil Company*

THE NEW YORK CONNECTION

Following the Civil War, New York City became the nation's center for making clothes. Its shops made coats, dresses, shirts, hats, boots, and shoes. By 1880, New York was the nation's leading industrial state. The cities and towns of upstate New York also experienced great industrial growth in this period. Buffalo and Binghamton became known for their fine iron products. Syracuse specialized in manufacturing machinery and tools. Corning became home to a famous glass company. Thomas A. Edison formed Edison General Electricity Company at Schenectady in 1889. This company later became General Electric. Rochester became a center for optics and photography.

Library of Congress

Thomas Alva Edison

FACTORS EXPLAINING NEW YORK'S INDUSTRIALIZATION

New York State had excellent transportation — railroads, canals, and roads. New York Harbor provided a safe port for shipping to other states or to Europe.

Large numbers of skilled and unskilled workers lived in New York.

Credit and loans were available from New York banks.

GREAT BUSINESS LEADERS: HEROES OR VILLAINS?

Business leaders played a crucial role in the rise of industry. Often they achieved their success by taking advantage of competitors and workers. Some of these business leaders became very wealthy, allowing them to have an important influence on American economic life.

ANDREW CARNEGIE (1835–1919)

Andrew Carnegie was a poor Scottish immigrant who became one of the world's richest men. He dominated the steel industry by selling steel at low prices and putting other steel companies out of business. Carnegie forced workers to put in long hours at low wages and stopped them from joining unions. Later in life, Carnegie gave large sums of money to education, public libraries and the arts.

Andrew Carnegie

Library of Congress

JOHN D. ROCKEFELLER (1839–1937)

John D. Rockefeller formed the Standard Oil Company. Because he controlled most of the oil refinery business, he was able to force railroad companies to give him special low rates for shipping oil, while they charged higher rates to his competitors. By 1900, Rockefeller had almost total control over the oil industry. Later in life he also gave money to education and science.

THE RISE OF BIG BUSINESS

Companies such as those owned by Carnegie and Rockefeller grew powerful by driving smaller competitors out of business. They lowered their prices until rival producers could not compete. In some cases, companies selling similar products made agreements to join together. As a result of these agreements, monopolies were created. The aim of a **monopoly** (*a company that controls all the business in an industry*) is to eliminate all competition and then raise its own prices. Consumers have no choice to buy elsewhere since there is only one seller.

THE RESPONSE OF GOVERNMENT TO MONOPOLISTIC PRACTICES

At first, most government leaders felt that allowing businesses to operate without interference would lead to the production of the best and cheapest goods. But the abuses of "big business" finally forced government to react. Congress passed two laws to deal with the situation:

★ **Interstate Commerce Act (1887)** made certain practices of railroad companies illegal, such as agreements with other railroad companies to control rates. A commission was created to ensure that the law was obeyed.

★ **Sherman Antitrust Act (1890)** prohibited certain tactics used by companies against their competitors. The act showed that Congress now felt something had to be done to stop the unfair practices of some big businesses.

THE RESPONSE OF LABOR

Although the Industrial Revolution brought increased profits to business people and more goods to consumers, workers often suffered. Industrialization created a larger workforce. Working conditions underwent great changes. Workers put in a six-day workweek, working ten to fourteen hours a day. Conditions were often hazardous — especially in factories and mines. The work was often boring, repetitive, and monotonous.

Trying to eliminate child labor in mines and factories was one reason for the development of labor unions

National Archives

Industrial workers found they had little power to raise their salaries or to improve their working conditions. Since much work required little skill, unskilled workers could easily be replaced. Eventually, some workers began organizing into **labor unions** to have more power than they did as individuals. If an employer refused union demands for higher pay, union members could walk off the job on **strike.**

KNIGHTS OF LABOR

Workers also tried to organize on a national level. The **Knights of Labor** was formed in 1869 as one large union that included both skilled and unskilled workers. The Knights demanded an 8-hour work day, higher wages, and safety codes for factories. After several losing strikes, the Knights fell apart. One reason for their failure was because skilled workers refused to be grouped in the same union as unskilled workers.

AMERICAN FEDERATION OF LABOR

The **American Federation of Labor** was founded in 1881 by **Samuel Gompers.** He hoped to create a powerful union by uniting workers with the same economic interests. Gompers brought together several small unions of skilled workers (*such as carpenters, cigar makers, shoemakers*) into a single national union. The A.F.L. emerged as the voice of organized labor in fighting for better working conditions, but it excluded unskilled workers.

 ## THE NEW YORK CONNECTION

One problem early unions faced was that government leaders favored businesses over unions. This feeling began to change after the **Triangle Shirtwaist Factory Fire.** In 1911, a fire killed 146 workers, mostly women, at this New York City factory. An investigation showed the workers could not escape because the doors were locked from the outside. As a result of this tragedy, the public demanded the government help workers, and new laws were passed.

Firefighters put out the flames at the Triangle Shirtwaist Factory

Jarrett Archives

URBANIZATION AND IMMIGRATION

In 1865, most Americans lived in the countryside. By 1920, half of all Americans lived in **urban** areas (*cities*) like Chicago and New York. This movement of people from rural areas to cities is known as **urbanization.**

 ## THE NEW YORK CONNECTION

By 1900, New York City's population stood at almost 3 ½ million people — more than the population of the entire state 50 years earlier. Other cities around the state were also growing rapidly. By 1910, Buffalo's population was ten times larger than it had been sixty years earlier.

REASONS FOR URBANIZATION

In the late 1800s, cities across the nation experienced a rapid growth in their population. There were a number of reasons why people flocked to cities. Many new factories and workshops attracted people in search of jobs. People were also drawn to the cultural aspects of city life, such as theatres, museums, and libraries. Many newcomers were farm-

Library of Congress

Chicago, 1915 — as cities grew, so did their problems

ers who had no work because new farm machinery had replaced them. In the late 1800s, immigrants from Europe began moving to American cities in growing numbers. By the 1900s, African Americans also began migrating from the South to large cities, especially in the North and Midwest, in search of a better life. As cities grew, new problems developed.

Inadequate Public Services. Cities lacked the ability to deliver increased public services — hospitals, police forces, schools, fire departments, street cleaning, and garbage collection.

Transportation. Horse-drawn coaches and later electric trolleys were needed to transport workers to their jobs. To eliminate the pollution created by coaches and trolleys, New York City built a **subway** in 1900. By 1930, New York City had the world's largest subway system.

THE PROBLEMS CREATED BY GROWING CITIES

Overcrowding. Families were crowded into **tenements** (*small apartment buildings*). These tenements often lacked daylight, fresh air, and adequate plumbing.

Corruption. Many cities were run by corrupt political bosses, like **Boss Tweed** in New York City, who promised jobs and services to immigrants in exchange for their votes.

Social Tensions. In the cities, rich people lived next door to the poor. Seeing the luxuries of the wealthy distressed poor people and increased social tensions.

THE IMMIGRATION EXPERIENCE

One reason cities grew so fast was because of the flood of immigrants. Immigrants came here because conditions in their own countries were poor and because they believed conditions in the United States would be better.

SHIFTING PATTERNS OF IMMIGRATION

In the first hundred years after independence, the United States had no laws limiting immigration. From 1607 to 1880, most immigrants to the United States came from Northern Europe. A great wave of Irish and German immigrants entered the United States between 1840 and 1890. Many settled in the Midwest. These English, Scots, Irish, Germans and Scandinavians became known as "**old immigrants.**" They brought many of their customs and traditions to America. There were also Chinese immigrants in the West, and Mexican-Americans in the states annexed from Mexico in 1848.

THE NEW IMMIGRANTS

The general pattern of immigration began to change in the 1880s. Immigrants now came from Southern and Eastern Europe — especially Poland, Italy, Austria-Hungary, Greece and Russia. They were often

Immigrant children often were the first in their family to learn English and become "Americanized"

Catholic and Jewish, rather than Protestant. These newcomers often were extremely poor, spoke little or no English, and dressed differently from other Americans. They often settled in **ghettos** — ethnic neighborhoods in cities like New York City, where they could continue speaking their own language. For example, Jewish immigrants spoke Yiddish in New York City's Lower East Side, and Italians in large numbers settled in "Little Italy." They often took work as unskilled laborers, working long hours for low wages. They frequently lived in crowded apartments and faced hostility from outsiders. These arrivals from Eastern and Southern Europe were referred to as "**new immigrants.**"

U.S. IMMIGRATION (1840–1920)
WHERE THEY CAME FROM:

SCANDINAVIA

RUSSIA

CANADA
1,800,000

1,950,000 3,280,000

GERMANY

UNITED STATES

GREAT BRITAIN & IRELAND
7,900,000

All Other European Countries

5,365,000

ITALY

790,000

4,100,000

MEXICO
230,000

AFRICA

ASIA

6,270,000

ATTEMPTS TO LIMIT IMMIGRATION

At the end of the 1800s, some Americans, referred to as **nativists,** spoke out against further immigration. Nativists feared the "new immigrants," with their foreign customs and languages, would never adjust to American society. They also feared that immigrants would take jobs from other Americans, since they were willing to work for less wages. The first immigration laws were directed against Asians. In the 1920s, Congress passed laws limiting European immigration.

★ **The Chinese Exclusion Act** (1882) and the **Gentlemen's Agreement** (1907) limited immigration from China and Japan.

★ **Immigration Acts of the 1920s.** In the 1920s, Congress established **quotas** which restricted immigration from Eastern and Southern Europe. These laws were passed in part because of prejudice against the "new immigrants."

THE SETTLEMENT OF THE FRONTIER

Cities were not the only places affected by the changes brought on by the Industrial Revolution. Settlement of the final **frontier** — the dividing line between areas occupied by **Native American Indian** peoples, and people from the U.S. and Europe — was also an effect of industrialization.

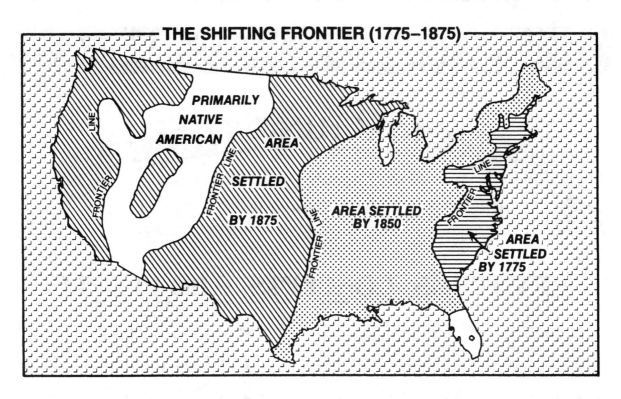

The last frontier consisted of the Great Plains and the Far West. The **Great Plains** were home to millions of buffalo and the Native American Indian tribes who lived off them. The completion of the transcontinental railroad in 1869 cut travel time to the West. It also made it possible for new ranchers and farmers to ship their cattle and grain to Eastern markets. The **Homestead Act** (1862), further encouraged the settlement of the West. This act gave settlers 160 acres of free land if they farmed it for five years. Within a short span of thirty years, from 1860 to 1890 — the herds of buffalo were destroyed, Native American Indians were forced onto **reservations** (*reserved lands set aside by the government*) and the Great Plains were divided up into farms and ranches.

The coming of the railroad put an end to the traditional way of life of Native American Indian tribes

Library of Congress

SUMMARIZING YOUR UNDERSTANDING

OVERARCHING THEME

After the Civil War, the United States began a process of transformation from a nation of farmers to one of the world's leading industrial powers.

KEY TERMS, CONCEPTS, AND PEOPLE

★ Scarcity

★ Free Market Economy

★ Industrial Revolution

★ Transcontinental Railroad

★ Corporations

★ Andrew Carnegie

★ John D. Rockefeller

★ American Federation of Labor

★ Samuel Gompers

★ Urbanization

TESTING YOUR UNDERSTANDING

MULTIPLE-CHOICE QUESTIONS

1   **A major result of the Industrial Revolution in the United States was**
   1   a decreased number of factories
   2   that people bought fewer goods
   3   a movement of people to cities
   4   a sharp increase in all prices

2   **The economic system of the United States in the late 1800s can best be described as**
   1   communism
   2   socialism
   3   mercantilism
   4   capitalism

3   Which would be a secondary source of information about the Industrial Revolution?

1   a textbook chapter written in 1940 on the Industrial Revolution
2   a diary of a factory owner written in 1880
3   a photograph of a child working in a factory in 1875
4   an immigrant's letter written in 1888 about factory conditions

4   In an outline, one of these is the main topic, and the other three are sub-topics. Which one is the main topic?

1   Causes of U.S. Industrialization   3   New Inventions & Technology
2   Population Growth   4   Expansion of Railroads

5   Which best describes why workers usually join labor unions?

1   to increase production levels   3   to lower consumer prices
2   to improve working conditions   4   to eliminate racial prejudice

Base your answer to question 6 on the table below.

THE GROWTH OF BUSINESSES IN AMERICA, 1870–1900

Year	Number of Businesses
1870	425,000
1875	600,000
1880	750,000
1885	925,000
1890	1,100,000
1895	1,200,000
1900	1,180,000

Source: *Historical Statistics of the United States*

6   Which conclusion can BEST be drawn from the information in the table?

1   Before the Civil War, many businesses were privately owned.
2   The population of the United States doubled between 1870 and 1890.
3   The period after the Civil War saw a dramatic increase in the number of businesses.
4   Before the Civil War, the corporation was the most popular form of business organization.

7 **The Knights of Labor and the American Federation of Labor were similar in that both sought**

   1   government ownership of industries   **3**   higher wages for managers

   2   a shorter workday for workers   **4**   a reduction in worker benefits

8 **Which event is correctly paired with one of its major effects?**

   1   American Revolution — abolition of slavery

   2   Civil War — women were given the right to vote

   3   Reconstruction — the United States achieved independence

   4   Industrial Revolution — the development of labor unions

9 **Which statement about the Sherman Antitrust Act is most accurate?**

   1   It gave states the power to control the federal budget.

   2   It sought to stop the growth of business monopolies.

   3   It led to the establishment of the Labor Department.

   4   It created the Interstate Commerce Commission.

10 **Which series of events is in correct chronological order?**

   1   Civil War → American Revolution → Knights of Labor

   2   Declaration of Independence → Bill of Rights → U.S. Constitution

   3   American Revolution → Civil War → Interstate Commerce Act

   4   Declaration of Independence → Homestead Act → Bill of Rights

11 **The movement of people from rural areas to cities is called**

   1   reconstruction   **3**   urbanization

   2   nativism   **4**   mercantilism

12 **Which statement about nativists is most accurate?**

   1   They wanted to end slavery.

   2   They opposed immigration from some areas.

   3   They favored unlimited immigration.

   4   They encouraged immigrants to settle in California.

13 **An experience shared by many "new immigrants" was that they**

   1   first settled in ethnic ghettos

   2   settled in farm areas where cheap land was available

   3   rapidly adopted mainstream lifestyles

   4   immediately enrolled in colleges to get free education

14 **A landless settler heading West in the 1860s in the United States would most likely have supported passage of the**

   1 Stamp Act   **3** Homestead Act

   2 Jim Crow laws   **4** Sherman Antitrust Act

CONSTRUCTED-RESPONSE QUESTION

Base your answers to questions 1 through 3 on the pie charts below.

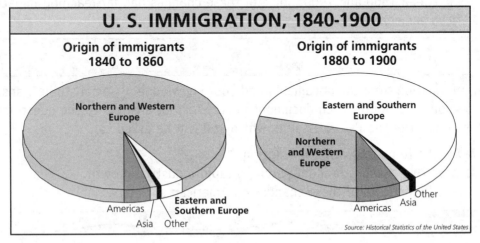

U. S. IMMIGRATION, 1840-1900

Origin of immigrants 1840 to 1860 — Northern and Western Europe, Americas, Asia, Other, Eastern and Southern Europe

Origin of immigrants 1880 to 1900 — Eastern and Southern Europe, Northern and Western Europe, Americas, Asia, Other

Source: Historical Statistics of the United States

1. Which area of the world did most immigrants to the United States come from during the years 1840–1860? _____

2. What changes, if any, occurred in Eastern and Southern European immigration to the United States between the years 1840–1860 and 1880–1900? _____

_____

3. Describe **one** way "new immigrants" to the United States differed from "old immigrants" already in the United States. _____

_____

DOCUMENT-BASED QUESTIONS: WRITING A DOCUMENT-BASED ESSAY

The **Grade 8 Intermediate Social Studies Test** requires you to answer a **document-based question.** This type of question tests your ability to interpret historical documents. Let's look at a typical document-based question:

This question is based on the accompanying documents (1-6). The question is designed to test your ability to work with historical documents. Some of the documents have been edited for the purpose of the question. As you analyze the documents, take into account both the source of each document and any point of view that may be presented in the document.

Historical Context:

As a result of the Industrial Revolution, the United States underwent dramatic changes between 1860 and 1900. Some of these changes had far-reaching impacts on American society.

Task:

Using information from the documents and your knowledge of social studies, answer the questions that follow each document in Part A. Your answers to the questions will help you write the Part B essay in which you will be asked to:

- *Define* the term "Industrial Revolution."
- *Describe* **two** changes brought about by rapid industrial growth.
- *Discuss* **two** effects of these changes on American society.

PART A: SHORT ANSWER

Directions: Analyze the documents and answer the short-answer questions that follow each document in the space provided.

DOCUMENT 1

In discussing the Industrial Revolution, it is easier to understand *what* happened than to determine *why* it happened. Historians are in agreement in describing the Industrial Revolution — the changes in industry and society that resulted from the introduction and large scale use of machinery to replace hand labor.

— Bernard Feder, *Viewpoints in American History*

1. How do historians define the Industrial Revolution? _____

_____ **[1]**

DOCUMENT 2

Farmers working the land, 1825

Farmers working the land, 1898

2a. Based on the first picture, what methods were used by farmers to raise crops in 1825? _____ **[2]**

2b. Based on the second photograph, what methods were used by farmers to raise crops in 1898? _____ **[2]**

DOCUMENT 3

3. This photograph was taken in the late1800s. What effects did industrialization have on these children? _____

_____ **[1]**

Children at work in a textile factory

DOCUMENT 4

Farm House, 1828
Floors: one
People per building: 3 to 5

Tenement, 1898
Floors: five or six
People per tenement: 200 to 400

4a. Based on the first photograph, how many people typically lived in a farm house in a wilderness area in 1828? _____ **[1]**

4b. Based on the second photograph, what was housing like for many people living in cities in 1898? _____ **[2]**

DOCUMENT 5

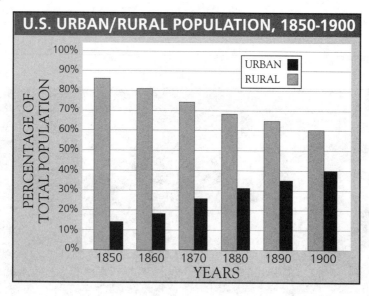

5. What happened to the percentage of people living in urban areas as a result of the Industrial Revolution? _____ **[1]**

DOCUMENT 6

> **Q.** What is the social air in a machinist's house? Is there evidence of happiness and joy, or is it somber and gloomy?
>
> **A.** Machinists have got to work ten hours a day, and they work very hard. When a man works that hard he's always cranky, and he makes those around cranky as well. So, instead of a pleasant home, he's always afraid of losing his job or that his wages will be reduced through competition, and facing starvation makes him sad. And of course the whole family is the same, so the house looks like a dull prison instead of a home.
>
> — *Testimony of a machinist before Congress, 1885*

6. Give two reasons why the machinist said machinists' homes are sad and gloomy.

_____ **[2]**

PART B: ESSAY

Directions: Write a well-organized essay that includes an introduction, several paragraphs, and a conclusion. Use evidence from at least **four** documents in the body of the essay. Support your response with relevant facts, examples, and details. Include additional outside information.

Historical Context:

As a result of the Industrial Revolution, the United States underwent dramatic changes between 1860 and 1900. Some of these changes had far-reaching impacts on American society.

Task:

Using information from the documents and your knowledge of social studies, write an essay in which you

- *Define* the term the Industrial Revolution.
- *Describe* **two** changes brought about by rapid industrial growth.
- *Discuss* **two** effects of these changes on American society.

To do well on a document-based question, you need to focus on three areas:

An easy way to remember this three-step approach is to use the first letter of each word and think of the word "**L•A•W.**" Let's apply this approach to answer the document-based question you just examined. We begin by looking at the documents.

"L"— LOOK AT THE DOCUMENTS

Document-based questions on the **Grade 8 Intermediate Test in Social Studies** are partially organized for you. It is important to thoroughly and carefully *answer all of the questions* in **PART A.** What you write in **PART A** will provide a basis for your essay answer in **PART B.**

In **PART A,** you will be presented with from 5 to 8 different documents. Each document will be followed by one or two questions. The documents will all be related to a single topic. In the model document-based question, all of the questions are related to the Industrial Revolution.

The question(s) accompanying each document will help you focus on what is most important about that document. The information you write for **PART A** will thus become the evidence you use to support your main ideas for **PART B.** Do not rush to answer each question. Instead, take a few moments to carefully look over the document. Look at the question and think about what it is directing you to focus on. Each question provides a clue about what the testmakers want you to get out of that document. Be aware that some documents may have more than just one correct answer.

"A" — ANALYZE THE DOCUMENTS

You are now ready for the second part of the "L•A•W" approach — to analyze the documents. Since a document-based question may have up to eight documents, you need a way to organize this information *before* you write your answer. One method that can be very helpful in arranging the documents is to use a **Document Box.**

WHAT IS A DOCUMENT BOX?

A **Document Box** is a table listing the documents and assigning columns for each "action word" used in the *Task.* For example, in the model question, the *Task* asked you to perform three different actions:

(1) *define* the Industrial Revolution

(2) *describe* two changes brought about by rapid industrial growth, and

(3) *discuss* two effects of these changes on American society.

In addition, the **Document Box** includes space for additional information based on your outside knowledge of social studies. For this sample question, your **Document Box** should therefore contain four columns and space for additional information:

Document	Industrial Revolution	Describe Changes	Discuss Effects
Additional Information: _____			

COMPLETING THE DOCUMENT BOX

Let's examine what you must do to complete each column of the **Document Box:**

★ In the *Document* column, you should list each document. Since this question has six documents, list 1 to 6 in the document column.

★ Next, you need to examine each document to see which part of the *Task* it can help you to answer. The question accompanying the document will usually direct you to what is important about it. For example:

• Document 1 provides a *definition* of the Industrial Revolution. Thus, in the ***Industrial Revolution*** column, you would place a ✔ alongside Document 1.

- Document 2 *describes* a change that occurred during the Industrial Revolution — farmers moved from raising crops by hand to using machines. In the *Changes* column, place a ✔ by Document 2.

- Document 4 can be used to answer two questions. The second picture shows that people began moving to cities — which was a major change brought about by the Industrial Revolution. Therefore, place a ✔ in the *Changes* column for Document 4. The picture also shows that conditions in cities became crowded and congested — an *effect* of the Industrial Revolution. You may recall that urbanization created a variety of other problems as well. Thus, also place a ✔ in the *Effects* column.

- Merely answering the questions in **PART A** and using that information in **PART B** will **not** be enough to earn full credit. You also have to provide additional outside information from your knowledge of social studies.

Document	Industrial Revolution	Describe Changes	Discuss Effects
1	✔		
2		✔	
3		✔	✔
4		✔	✔
5		✔	✔
6			✔

Additional Information: *Children were often used instead of adults to work in factories because they were paid less money and could do jobs requiring small hands. Working in factories all day, they missed sunshine and fresh air.*

(Relates to both *Changes* and *Effects*)

To receive a top score of 4 or 5, you must *analyze* as well as *describe*. You must apply information from the documents and from your outside knowledge to support or evaluate your thesis statement.

"W" —WRITE THE ESSAY

Your answers to **PART A** and the information you have organized in your **Document Box** will serve as the basis of your **PART B** answer.

In writing your essay answer, you should remember to follow the same rules as you would for writing any good essay, except that you now must include references to the documents in your answer. To help you organize your answer, imagine your answer as a hamburger consisting of a **top bun, patties of meat,** and a **bottom bun:**

TOP BUN (INTRODUCTION)

You need to introduce your reader to your essay by identifying the historical context. The historical context sets the time and place for your essay. It is acceptable to use information from the question about the context, but be sure to use your own words. Next, you need a clear statement of what you will be writing about. A **thesis statement** identifies what you are trying to show in your essay answer.

PATTIES OF MEAT (MAIN PARAGRAPHS)

The main part of your answer consists of the "patties of meat" — the main ideas and supporting details that answer the *Task.* Each paragraph in the body of your answer should correspond to a bulleted item in the *Task.* The **Document Box** is where you have already organized your main ideas and supporting details. Each column devoted to a bulleted item should provide the basis for a topic sentence for each paragraph in the body of your essay. Use the document and answers you wrote to the accompanying questions for your facts and supporting details. Don't just describe or quote from the documents. You must draw conclusions on how they relate to your thesis.

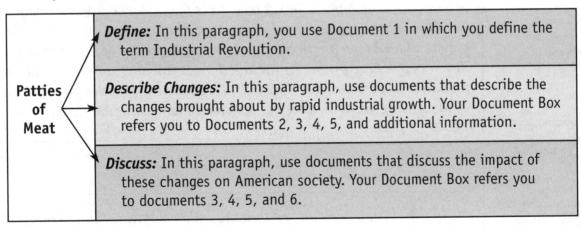

Patties of Meat

Define: In this paragraph, you use Document 1 in which you define the term Industrial Revolution.

Describe Changes: In this paragraph, use documents that describe the changes brought about by rapid industrial growth. Your Document Box refers you to Documents 2, 3, 4, 5, and additional information.

Discuss: In this paragraph, use documents that discuss the impact of these changes on American society. Your Document Box refers you to documents 3, 4, 5, and 6.

BOTTOM BUN (CONCLUSION)

The "bottom bun" is used to close your essay. A conclusion is simply a final summary of what you have stated in the main body of your essay. It can be introduced with such words as "therefore" or "In conclusion."

Let's examine what a model answer to the question might look like:

Your introduction restates the historical context.

Your thesis statement introduces the reader to the body of the essay.

This part of the paragraph draws on information you provided in answer to Part A.

Your topic sentence for this paragraph.

Notice how the answer mentions two changes and provides additional information.

Your topic sentence for this part of the essay.

You complete the information for this essay.

Your conclusion summarizes what you have stated in your essay.

As a result of the Industrial Revolution, Americans experienced some of the most dramatic changes in their history. This essay will examine what the Industrial Revolution was, the changes it brought about, and some of the ways it affected American society.

The Industrial Revolution is a term historians have used to identify certain changes in American industry and society. These changes resulted from the greater use of machinery instead of hand labor. The Industrial Revolution began with the steam engine and moved to electricity and other sources of power.

The Industrial Revolution brought many important changes to our nation. For example, early in the 1800s farm work was done mainly by hand and animal power. However, as Document 2 shows, by the 1880s farmers were able to use steam-powered machines to work the land, making them far more efficient. More land could by cultivated and yields from the land were greater. A second important change brought about by the Industrial Revolution was that people began to work in factories. Document 3 provides evidence of what factory work was like for some children. Children were often employed instead of adults in factories because they worked for less money. Children working in factories could do jobs requiring small hands, but they were denied sunshine and fresh air.

The Industrial Revolution also brought many significant effects in America. One important effect of the Industrial Revolution was the urbanization of American society. Less farm workers were needed because of farm machinery. People started moving to cities from the countryside. As people flooded into cities, a variety of new problems developed. These problems included overcrowding, poor sanitation facilities, and a shortage of schools. Document 4 provides an example of the type of overcrowding that existed in tenement homes. A second effect of industrialization was _____

_____

_____

In conclusion, we can see that the Industrial Revolution changed the way goods were produced—from the home to the factory, and how goods were produced—from hand to machine labor. These changes in the way goods were produced had many further effects, like urbanization and overcrowding. Some of these changes had a great effect on American society.

CHAPTER 9

FROM PROGRESSIVISM TO THE NEW DEAL,
From 1898 to 1941

In this chapter, you will learn about the United States in the first half of the twentieth century. Americans came to terms with some of the problems of industrial society — unemployment, unsafe working conditions, and political corruption. At the same time, the nation began playing a greater role in world affairs. In this chapter you will learn about the following:

State Archives of Michigan

U.S. soldiers fighting in World War I

★ **Progressive Movement.** Progressive reformers sought to end political corruption and to remedy social problems caused by industrialization. Presidents Roosevelt and Wilson introduced many Progressive reforms.

★ **U.S. Foreign Policy, 1898–1918.** The United States showed it was a world power by going to war with Spain in 1898. After the war, Americans acquired a colonial empire in the Caribbean, Asia, and the Pacific. In 1917, they entered World War I, helping to win that conflict.

★ **Prosperity and Depression.** In the 1920s, new technologies contributed to prosperity. When the New York Stock Market crashed in October 1929, millions of people were thrown out of work. President Franklin D. Roosevelt introduced the "New Deal" to revive the economy.

In studying this period, you should focus on the following questions:

★ What changes were brought about by the Progressive Movement?

★ How did the Spanish-American War lead to foreign policy changes?

★ Why did the United States enter World War I?

★ What factors led to the Great Depression?

MAJOR THEMES IN U.S. HISTORY: FOREIGN POLICY

WHAT IS FOREIGN POLICY?

Foreign policy is the conduct of one nation towards other nations. The main objective of American foreign policy has always been to promote our national interests. Many factors determine what those interests are.

National Security. One major goal is to protect our country from attack. Americans achieve this through military preparedness, responding to aggression, allying with friendly nations, and participating in international organizations.

Protection of U.S. Citizens, Investments, and Trade. Our government acts to protect American citizens and investments overseas. It also adopts policies that promote our economy.

THE GOALS OF U.S. FOREIGN POLICY

Promotion of Democracy. The United States actively seeks to spread its political system — democracy — to others.

Promotion of Human Rights and International Peace. The United States supports morality in both national and international affairs.

WHO MAKES FOREIGN POLICY?

Our Constitution gives control of foreign policy to the federal government. To prevent any one branch of the federal government from becoming too strong, the Constitution divided control of foreign policy between the President and Congress. The Constitution forces them to work together in making foreign policy.

President Franklin D. Roosevelt goes before Congress to ask for a declaration of war against Japan

Franklin D. Roosevelt Library

Newspapers, television, and radio are very influential in shaping foreign policy, since they decide what foreign news to report. The President and Congress are very sensitive to public opinion, since they know it was the public who elected them.

President Kennedy speaks to a crowd as the press takes notes

MILESTONES OF U.S. FOREIGN POLICY

Our national government has followed a variety of foreign policies in its relations with other nations. On the **Grade 8 Intermediate Social Studies Test,** you may be asked about one or more of these policies. The following chart briefly summarizes some of the major milestones of American foreign policy.

MILESTONE	DESCRIPTION
Washington's Farewell Address (1796)	President Washington advised Americans to avoid entangling alliances with European nations. This policy helped the United States keep out of war with France or England until 1812.
War of 1812	In 1812, Congress declared war against the British to stop the impressment of American sailors. Sometimes called the "Second War for Independence," Americans preserved their freedom. The war ended in December 1814.
Monroe Doctrine (1823)	President Monroe announced America would oppose attempts by European powers to reconquer former colonies that had become independent. Later, the doctrine was used by the United States to justify its interference in the Caribbean.
Manifest Destiny (early 1800s)	Many Americans believed the U.S. should expand to the Pacific coast. The desire for expansion led to the Mexican-American War in which Mexico lost a large part of its territory.
Spanish-American War (1898)	After the sinking of the *Maine,* Americans went to war with Spain to help Cuba win its independence. After winning the war, the U.S. gained the Philippines and other colonial possessions, such as Puerto Rico.

John F. Kennedy Presidential Library

MILESTONE	DESCRIPTION
American Imperialism (1898–early1900s)	After the Spanish-American War, America became an imperialist power by annexing the Philippines, Puerto Rico, Hawaii, and Samoa. Americans also developed trade with China and Japan.
Panama Canal and the "Big Stick Policy" (1902–1914)	Theodore Roosevelt reached an agreement with a newly independent Panama to build the Panama Canal. Later, President Roosevelt used his "Big Stick Policy" to bring the Caribbean region under U.S. control.
World War I (1917–1918)	Events in Europe led to war in 1914. At first America remained neutral. America entered the war in 1917 after Germans submarines attacked American ships in the Atlantic. American entry led to Allied victory by 1918.
Fourteen Points and Treaty of Versailles (1918–1919)	President Wilson announced U.S. war aims in the Fourteen Points, creating a basis for ending the war. He also proposed an international peace organization. Many of Wilson's ideas, including the League of Nations, were accepted in the Treaty of Versailles, but the U.S. Senate rejected the treaty.
Isolationism (1919–1941)	After World War I, Americans retreated into "isolationism" and attempted to avoid involvement in foreign alliances and wars. They also raised tariff rates and restricted immigration.
World War II (1939–1945)	World War II broke out when Germany invaded Poland. At first, Americans were neutral. In 1941, Japan attacked Pearl Harbor, bringing the United States into the war. The war ended in 1945, after Americans dropped atomic bombs on two Japanese cities.
The Cold War (1946–1989)	After World War II, America and the Soviet Union emerged as superpowers. When the Soviets established Communist governments in Eastern Europe, the "Cold War" began. Although both powers never went to war with each other, they stockpiled nuclear weapons and became involved in regional crises.
Korean War (1950–1953)	In 1950, Communist North Korea invaded South Korea. U.S. troops were sent to South Korea to repel the North Korean attack. When U.S. forces entered North Korea, Communist China also entered the war. After three years of fighting, a truce was signed leaving Korea exactly as before the war.
Vietnam War (1964–1973)	After achieving independence, North Vietnam began a war against the non-Communist South to reunite the country under Communist rule. Half a million U.S. troops were sent to aid South Vietnam, but they were unable to defeat the North Vietnamese and Vietcong. America finally withdrew.
The Persian Gulf War (1990)	Iraqi dictator Saddam Hussein invaded Kuwait. President Bush, with U.N. support, launched an invasion of Kuwait and Iraq, forcing an Iraqi withdrawal. The allies were able to liberate Kuwait, but ended the war without toppling Saddam Hussein in Iraq.
The "War on Terror" (2001–Present)	When al-Qaeda terrorists crashed two hijacked planes into the World Trade Center and one into the Pentagon, President G.W. Bush declared a "War on Terror." U.S. and allied troops toppled the Taliban in Afghanistan for shielding terrorists and Saddam Hussein in Iraq to prevent him from aiding terrorists.

MAJOR HISTORICAL DEVELOPMENTS

THE PROGRESSIVE MOVEMENT, 1900–1920

THE GRANGE AND POPULIST MOVEMENTS

In the 1870s, a majority of Americans still lived on farms. The settling of the Great Plains and use of machinery made farms much more productive, leading to overproduction. Although food prices began to fall, farmers' expenses remained high. Many farmers fell into debt. Some blamed their problems on the high prices charged by railroads to ship crops.

A PARTY OF PATCHES.
Grand Balloon Ascension—Cincinnati, May 20th, 1891.

This cartoon labels the Populists as a group of dreamers and radicals

Library of Congress

THE GRANGERS AND THE POPULIST PARTY, 1867–1896

In 1867, farmers organized the **Grange Movement** to deal with their problems. In several Midwest states, Grangers elected candidates who passed laws to control railroad rates. These laws were struck down by the Supreme Court, but Congress passed the **Interstate Commerce Act** to stop railroad abuses. In 1892, farmers joined forces with a new political party, the **Populist Party.** The Populists represented farmers, laborers and factory workers against banking and railroad interests.

POPULIST PARTY PROPOSALS	
Unlimited Coinage of Silver — Allow farm prices to rise through cheaper money, making loan repayments easier.	**Direct Election of Senators** — Have voters instead of state legislatures elect U.S. Senators.
Secret Ballot — Allow people to cast their votes in secret.	**Graduated Income Tax** — Directly tax wealthy individuals at a higher rate.
Restricted Immigration — Place quotas on future immigration.	**Shorter Work Day** — Give workers an eight-hour work day.

In 1896, the Democratic Party nominated **William Jennings Bryan** for President. Bryan adopted much of the Populist program, but lost the election in 1896 and again in 1900 to Republican candidate **William McKinley.** Bryan's defeats and better times for farmers brought an end to the Populist Party.

THE PROGRESSIVE MOVEMENT EMERGES

The **Progressive Movement** developed between 1900 and the start of World War I. Unlike the Populists, the Progressives were mainly middle-class reformers who lived in cities. The aim of the Progressives was to correct the political and economic abuses that resulted from America's rapid industrialization. Progressives wanted to use the power of government to stop these abuses.

MUCKRAKERS AND SOCIAL REFORMERS

Among the early Progressives were a group of newspaper reporters and writers known as **muckrakers.** The muckrakers wrote about the corrupt practices of big business and government. For example, writer **Upton Sinclair** described the unsanitary practices of the meat packing-industry in his novel *The Jungle*. Social reformers, like **Jane Addams,** established settlement houses that took care of the needs of immigrants and the poor.

Jane Addams

Corbis-Bettman Archives

 THE NEW YORK CONNECTION

New Yorkers also played leading roles in the Progressive Movement. **Jacob Riis** examined conditions of the urban poor in his book, *How the Other Half Lives* (1890). **W.E.B. DuBois** and other reformers met in New York City in 1909, where they founded the **NAACP** (*National Association for the Advancement of Colored People*). Its goal was to achieve full civil rights for African Americans.

ATTEMPTS TO REFORM GOVERNMENT AND POLITICS

To fight social abuses, Progressives believed it was important to reform government, which had been corrupted by big business and political bosses. Many Progressive candidates were elected to positions in local and state government, where they introduced reforms to make government more responsive to people's needs and less corrupt.

Secret Ballot. Voters now marked their ballots without their names, making them less subject to pressure and intimidation.

Election Reforms. In some states, voters gained the right to introduce bills directly into the state legislature. Some voters could also show their support for a bill by voting on whether or not they wanted it passed. Lastly, in some states elected officials could be removed from office by voters in a special election.

PROGRESSIVE REFORMS

Direct Election of Senators. The Constitution originally gave state legislatures the power to elect U.S. Senators. The **17th Amendment** (1913) changed the Constitution to make Senators elected directly by the people.

Direct Party Primaries. Party leaders began holding special elections (*primaries*) to determine who should be nominated by their party. This allowed party members, not political bosses, to control the selection of party candidates.

THE PROGRESSIVE PRESIDENTS

Presidents Theodore Roosevelt and Woodrow Wilson used the powers of the Presidency to introduce Progressive ideas at the national level.

★ **Theodore Roosevelt, 1901–1910.** Roosevelt put Progressive beliefs into action at the federal level by launching the break-up of Rockefeller's Standard Oil Company. This company controlled most of the oil industry. Roosevelt also acted to pass the **Pure Food and Drug Act** and the **Meat Inspection Act** in 1906, creating a system for government inspection of foods, meats and drugs sold to the public. He also promoted the conservation of wildlife areas on federal lands.

President Roosevelt is shown as defending the public against bad trusts

Library of Congress

★ **Woodrow Wilson, 1913–1921.** Like Roosevelt, Wilson used his power as President to control big business and to improve living conditions in America. An amendment to the Constitution allowed Congress to introduce a graduated income tax, requiring the rich to pay a higher percentage of their income in tax than less well-off Americans. Wilson also introduced the **Federal Reserve Act** of 1913. The act established a system of Federal Reserve Banks to regulate money and the banking industry by fixing the amount of money banks could lend.

Bureau of Engraving and Printing

Woodrow Wilson

THE WOMEN'S SUFFRAGE MOVEMENT

In the middle 1800s, men still held most positions of authority in society. Women began to organize in a struggle for equality.

Legally. Women were denied full equality of citizenship. They lacked the right to vote, to serve on juries, and to hold public office.	**Socially.** Women were expected to care for their home and children. They received little schooling. In fact, almost no colleges were willing to accept women.

HOW WOMEN WERE TREATED IN THE 1800s

Economically. Once a woman married, her husband usually took control of her income and property. Women were paid less than men for the same work. Higher paying jobs were not open to women.

 THE NEW YORK CONNECTION

To bring about change, women began to organize. Among the leaders for women's rights were **Lucretia Mott** and **Elizabeth Cady Stanton.** In 1848, they helped organize a women's rights meeting in Seneca Falls, New York to "discuss the social, civil, and religious rights of women." The **Seneca Falls Convention,** which passed resolutions that women were equal to men, is often seen as the start of the **Women's Rights Movement.**

By the late 1800s, the chief goal of the movement was **suffrage** — winning the right to vote. Elizabeth Cady Stanton and **Susan B. Anthony** led the campaign to win this right. During World War I, millions of women filled male jobs in factories, mills and mines. After the war, it was harder than ever to deny that women were the equals of men. The **Nineteenth Amendment** was passed in 1920, prohibiting states from denying any citizen the right to vote on the basis of gender.

Susan B. Anthony (standing) and Elizabeth Cady Stanton

THE PROGRESSIVE MOVEMENT COMES TO AN END

In 1917, Americans entered World War I. Women's suffrage and the prohibition of alcoholic drinks were both passed soon after the war. These were the final reforms of the Progressive Era. The best Progressive ideas had been made into law. As Americans turned their attention to the prosperity of the 1920s, progressivism lost any further appeal.

After World War I, women finally achieved the right to vote throughout the nation

U.S. FOREIGN POLICY, 1898–1918

During the late 1800s, the United States emerged as a major world power.

THE SPANISH-AMERICAN WAR OF 1898

Cuba, 90 miles off the coast of Florida, was one of Spain's last colonial possessions in Latin America. In 1894, Cubans rebelled to obtain their independence. Spain brutally crushed the rebellion. Several factors led the United States to intervene:

CAUSES OF THE SPANISH-AMERICAN WAR

Humanitarian Concerns. Americans felt they had a moral obligation to help the Cuban people in their struggle for independence from Spain.

Yellow Journalism. In the 1890s, several U.S. newspapers (especially those of Hearst and Pulitzer) deliberately sensationalized news from Cuba with stories of atrocities to sell more papers. Americans felt obliged to help the Cubans against Spanish brutality.

Economic Interests. The U.S. government wanted to protect American investments in Cuba and to prevent interruption of U.S. trade with Cuba.

Sinking of the *Maine*. The U.S. battleship *Maine* was blown up in Cuba's Havana harbor. Newspapers blamed the explosion on Spanish sabotage, leading to the declaration of war.

The Spanish-American War lasted less than four months. The Spanish were no match for the superior American forces. The Spanish-American War signaled the emergence of the United States as a world power. American forces quickly defeated Spanish troops in Cuba and Puerto Rico and the Spanish navy in the Philippines. The United States took over the Philippines, Guam, and Puerto Rico from Spain. Cuba became independent.

Sinking of the battleship Maine was an important reason for the war against Spain

Library of Congress

AMERICA BUILDS A COLONIAL EMPIRE

The United States went from being a nation without colonies to controlling a far-flung overseas empire. Some Americans felt it was wrong to force colonial rule on others, especially since Americans had once suffered under colonial rule at the hands of the British. Some Americans felt colonial rule violated the democratic principles of self-government. On the other hand, most Americans supported the new policy of **imperialism** (*the control of one country by another*).

Economic Reasons. The United States was now an industrial power. Colonies would provide raw materials for factories and markets to sell goods.	**Belief in Moral Superiority.** Many Americans believed they were a superior race and had a moral obligation to extend their way of life to others.

REASONS FOR OVERSEAS EXPANSION

Desire to be a Great Power. Some people believed that to be a powerful nation, the United States needed overseas colonies to provide naval bases. Otherwise, rival powers would gain control of these strategic places.

In 1898, the United States annexed Hawaii. It also held onto the Philippines, despite the armed resistance of many Filipinos.

AMERICAN INVOLVEMENT IN THE PACIFIC

American trade with China and Japan increased after the United States gained the Philippines, Hawaii, and Guam. These islands served as fueling stations for American steamships crossing the Pacific Ocean.

A Chinese "Boxer"

Library of Congress

★ **Japan.** Japan's rulers had blocked contact with other countries for nearly 200 years. In 1853, **Commodore Matthew Perry** was sent to Japan to demand that it open itself to trade with the United States. Fearing Western military power, Japan gave in. After opening their doors to the world, Japan quickly learned to adopt Western ideas and technology.

★ **China.** In 1899, Americans grew concerned that European powers were taking over China and cutting off U.S. trade. In reaction, the United States announced the **"Open Door Policy."** It stated that all nations should have equal trading rights in China. The next year, a Chinese group called the "Boxers" opposed Western intervention and began attacking foreigners. After the **Boxer Rebellion** was crushed, the U.S. acted to stop China from being carved up by the European powers.

AMERICAN INVOLVEMENT IN THE CARIBBEAN

After the Spanish-American War, the United States also gained direct control of Puerto Rico and indirect control of Cuba. In 1904, President Theodore Roosevelt declared that the United States would act as a policeman in the Western Hemisphere. He believed the United States had to act to keep European powers out, to promote U.S. investment and trade. This expansion of power in Latin America became known as the **Roosevelt Corollary** or "**Big Stick Policy**." Roosevelt and later Presidents repeatedly sent troops to countries in the West Indies and Central America.

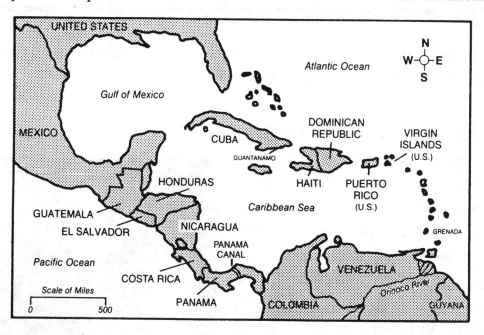

★ **The Panama Canal.** Americans recognized the need to build a canal between the Atlantic and Pacific Oceans to shorten the trip from the east to the west coast. At the time, Panama was a province of Colombia, a country in South America. In 1903, President Theodore Roosevelt helped Panamanian rebels win independence from Colombia in exchange for the right to build and control the Panama Canal. Protection of the canal became a major strategic interest of the United States.

Teddy Roosevelt sits at a steam shovel as the Panama Canal is dug

THE UNITED STATES IN WORLD WAR I

Americans had traditionally followed a policy of non-involvement in European affairs. But developments in transportation and communication brought distant parts of the world closer. Trade with Europe and concern for the future of democracy eventually brought Americans into the war.

THE OUTBREAK OF WAR IN EUROPE, 1914

Struggles among European nations, intense national-ism, and a system of alliances led to the outbreak of war in Europe. When a member of Austria-Hungary's

National Archives

German soldiers advance along the front, August 1914

ruling family was assassinated, Austria invaded Serbia in retaliation. Russia entered the conflict to help Serbia. Next, Germany came to the aid of Austria-Hungary. France and Great Britain joined as allies of Russia. Within a few weeks, all of Europe was at war.

THE UNITED STATES BECOMES INVOLVED, 1917

When war first broke out, President Wilson attempted to follow the traditional policy of **neutrality.** Despite his best efforts, Americans eventually became involved in the war.

REASONS FOR U.S. INVOLVEMENT IN WORLD WAR I

Ties with Allies. A common language and history tied Americans to Britain. The United States, Great Britain, and France also shared the same democratic political system, while Britain was a major trading partner.

German Actions. Americans were shocked at Germany's invasion of neutral Belgium. Publication of the **Zimmerman Telegram,** a secret German message offering to help Mexico against the United States, further angered Americans.

German Use of Submarine Warfare. Germany began to sink ships carrying goods to Britain. This violated "**freedom of the seas**" — the principle that neutrals have a right to ship non-war goods to nations at war. When German submarines attacked unarmed U.S. ships, Congress declared war on Germany.

THE UNITED STATES AT WAR, 1917–1918

Once war was declared, it was supported by a majority of Americans. President Wilson announced that the war was being fought to "save the world for democracy." Congress gave Wilson sweeping powers to control businesses and workers. A military draft brought millions of soldiers into the army. Women and African Americans joined the workforce to replace men sent overseas and to produce war goods.

THE PEACE SETTLEMENT

President Wilson announced America's war aims in the **Fourteen Points.** They called for freedom of the seas, reduced armaments, and an end to secret treaties between nations. Wilson also proposed creation of a **League of Nations** to peacefully settle future disputes between countries. Germany surrendered in November 1918. Many of the terms of the final

President Wilson (far right) and other allied leaders at the peace conference in Paris

peace settlement, known as the **Versailles Treaty,** were very different from those proposed in Wilson's Fourteen Points. The Versailles Treaty was quite harsh on Germany. Germany had to pay reparations to the Allies for starting the war. The treaty also adopted Wilson's idea of a League of Nations.

AMERICA REFUSES TO JOIN THE LEAGUE OF NATIONS

Wilson hoped the League would provide a place for nations to discuss their problems rather than going to war. According to the U.S. Constitution, all treaties had to be approved by the Senate. The Senate, fearing Americans would be drawn into another foreign war, rejected the treaty. The refusal of the United States to join the League marked America's return to a policy of **isolationism** (*refusing to become involved in the affairs of other countries*). In the 1920s, Americans kept away from involvement in European affairs, raised tariff rates, and restricted immigration to the United States.

THE ROARING TWENTIES, 1920–1929

After World War I ended, rising standards of living resulted in the growth of the middle class, an increase in single-family homes, and the development of suburbs. Working conditions and wages improved, while women entered the workforce in larger numbers. But not all groups shared in this prosperity.

FACTORS UNDERLYING THE PROSPERITY OF THE 1920s

Rise of the Automobile.
In the 1920s, auto ownership jumped from 7 to 23 million. This enormous growth in automobile ownership stimulated other industries — such as steel, glass, and rubber. By 1929, one of every nine workers was employed in an auto-related industry.

Development of Other Industries.
The use of electricity created new household products — vacuum cleaners, refrigerators, and toasters. These new products created jobs, and produced large profits for many companies.

Improved Production.
New production techniques were applied to manufacturing. The **assembly line** (*where workers stayed in one place as products came to them on a conveyor belt*), and other labor-saving devices made American industry more efficient and productive.

Government Policies.
From 1920 to 1932, three Republican Presidents — Harding, Coolidge and Hoover — followed policies favoring business. Each believed in **laissez-faire capitalism:** that government should interfere as little as possible in the affairs of business.

CULTURAL VALUES IN CONFLICT

The spread of automobiles, changes brought about by electricity, and new scientific discoveries had a deep impact on American society. The 1920s saw the appearance of new and conflicting values. Women felt more confident than ever before and wore new clothes and hairstyles that reflected their independence. Young people experienced greater freedom, which affected literature, art, and fashion. More leisure time gave people greater opportunity for entertainment. Americans worshipped new heroes like baseball great **Babe Ruth**, **Charles Lindbergh** (*the first person to fly solo across the Atlantic*), and **Amelia Earhart** (*who disappeared in a daring attempt to fly solo around the world*).

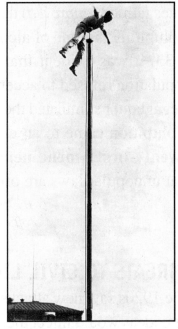

Wild fads, like flagpole sitting, were popular during the 1920s

Library of Congress

THE NEW YORK CONNECTION

In the early twentieth century, large numbers of African Americans migrated from the South to the cities of the North. The center of African-American cultural life in the 1920s was Harlem in New York City. African Americans expressed new pride in their culture during what became known as the "**Harlem Renaissance.**" African-Americans poets like **Langston Hughes** and **Countee Cullen** expressed a new sense of independence, while jazz music became popular across the nation.

Many African-American families moved North in search of better jobs

Many reformers saw liquor as the main cause of poverty, crime, and the breakdown of families. In 1919, states ratified (*approved*) the **Eighteenth Amendment,** prohibiting the sale of alcoholic drinks. However, by 1933, it was evident that an increasing part of the population refused to accept the ban. The demand for illegal liquor stimulated the growth of organized crime. Prohibition came to an end with the passage of the **Twenty-first Amendment.** This experience showed that unpopular laws are often unenforceable.

By 1933, Americans tired of government officials destroying alcoholic beverages

THREATS TO CIVIL LIBERTIES

The 1920s saw new attacks on some people's rights. Many Americans feared that foreign ideas would infect the nation. Immigrants and racial minorities frequently became the targets of hostility. One reason for such attacks was the **Red Scare** — a fear that Communism (*which took over Russia in 1917*) would take over the United States.

Thousands of people suspected of being Communists were arrested in 1919-1920. African Americans also became the victims of mob lynchings. The **Ku Klux Klan** reemerged during the 1920s. Klan members were hostile to African Americans, Catholics, Jews, and immigrants and often acted violently against them.

AMERICA IN THE GREAT DEPRESSION, 1929–1940

Economies often go through good and bad periods. Economists refer to these up-and-down periods as the "**business cycle.**" In good times, businesses are growing and it is easy to find a job. The bad times are called **depressions,** when many businesses close down and people lose their jobs. The **Great Depression** was the worst such depression in American history. It began with the Stock Market Crash of 1929, and lasted throughout the 1930s.

National Archives

Makeshift huts were homes for the homeless during the Great Depression

CAUSES OF THE GREAT DEPRESSION

There were a several underlying causes of the Great Depression:

CAUSES OF THE GREAT DEPRESSION
Overproduction. The 1920s saw rapid increases in the production of new goods like cars and radios. Manufacturers were making more goods than Americans could afford to buy.
Shaky Banking. In the 1920s the government did not regulate banks. Bankers often invested depositors' money in unsound investments. Consumers bought more than they could afford. Many people could not pay their debts.
Stock Market Speculation. As stock prices rose in the 1920s, more and more people bought stocks, hoping to get rich quick. People bought stocks on credit, promising to pay the rest later. When the market crashed, many could not pay.

THE STOCK MARKET CRASH OF 1929

In October 1929, stock prices suddenly fell. People tried to sell their stocks but no one wanted to buy them. After the crash, people had no money to spend, and many businesses could not sell their goods. Some businesses were forced to shut down. As people lost their jobs, they had even less money to spend, leading to more businesses failures and forcing even more people out of work.

THE DUST BOWL

In the Great Plains, farmers were affected by a series of droughts. Crops dried up and the soil turned to dust. Farmers, unable to pay their mortgages, had to leave their farms. Over one million farmers were driven from their lands by the "dust bowl," and became migrant farm workers in California.

This scene of fertile farm land turned to dust was repeated throughout the Great Plains in the 1930s

FRANKLIN D. ROOSEVELT AND THE NEW DEAL

President **Herbert Hoover** felt that the federal government should not directly interfere in the economy. He believed private organizations could provide enough help. Hoover eventually changed his mind, but his programs provided too little, too late. Many Americans became frustrated when Hoover failed to act.

THE NATION TURNS TO FRANKLIN D. ROOSEVELT

By 1932, more than 13 million people were jobless, thousands stood on bread lines waiting for a meal, banks were failing, and thousands of people were losing their homes and farms. In the 1932 election, candidate **Franklin D. Roosevelt** promised new programs to put people back to work. Roosevelt, the New York State governor, easily defeated Hoover in the election and immediately took steps to get people back to work. He called his program the "**New Deal**." The New Deal established the idea that the federal government has a major responsibility for making sure that the nation's economy runs smoothly. Roosevelt explained his New Deal in terms of three "R's":

★ **Relief** measures were short-term steps to tide people over until the economy recovered. In those days, there was no unemployment insurance. Many Americans were without food or shelter and needed immediate help.

*During the New Deal, the **Civilian Conservation Corps** (1933) gave young people jobs.*

★ **Recovery** measures helped restore the economy by rebuilding people's purchasing power. These measures included the **National Recovery Administration** (1933), which promoted recovery codes for businesses. The codes set prices, placed limits on production, and established a minimum wage.

★ **Reform** measures sought to correct defects to ensure that such a severe depression would never strike again. New laws prevented abuses in the stock market and in banking. The most important of these measures was the **Social Security Act** (1935). It established funds to help Americans in case of disability, unemployment, or old age.

Although popular, the New Deal was controversial. Critics said the federal government was becoming too powerful and taxes were too high. Supporters felt this government action was needed to restore economic prosperity.

ROOSEVELT'S COURT-PACKING SCHEME

In 1935–36, the Supreme Court ruled two New Deal programs to be unconstitutional. Roosevelt feared the Court might declare other programs unconstitutional. In 1937, he proposed expanding the court by appointing enough new justices to give him a majority on the Court. Many saw the plan as an attempt to control the judiciary. Congress voted down the plan. Although Roosevelt failed to "pack" the court, the Supreme Court stopped overturning New Deal legislation.

Newspapers had a field day poking fun at Roosevelt's court-packing scheme

SUMMARIZING YOUR UNDERSTANDING

OVERARCHING THEME

*In the early 20th century,
the federal government grew in power as it helped
Americans deal with the problems of industrial society.*

KEY TERMS, CONCEPTS, AND PEOPLE

★ The Progressive Movement

★ Muckrakers

★ Theodore Roosevelt

★ Woodrow Wilson

★ Susan B. Anthony

★ Spanish American War

★ Harlem Renaissance

★ Great Depression

★ Franklin D. Roosevelt

★ New Deal

TESTING YOUR UNDERSTANDING

MULTIPLE-CHOICE QUESTIONS

1   A major aim of both the Grange and Populist Movements was to
   1   have government take ownership of private property
   2   require the national government to end inflation
   3   help farmers overcome their problems
   4   support the unlimited immigration of Asians

2   During the Progressive Era, Muckrakers sought to
   1   fight corruption in American society by publicly exposing it
   2   limit government controls on the economy
   3   increase the spirit of patriotism
   4   give more aid to people in less developed nations

3   **The direct election of Senators, the graduated income tax, and the use of primaries were all steps introduced during the**

   1   American Revolution

   2   Civil War

   3   Progressive Era

   4   New Deal

4   **A major concern of the Progressives was to**

   1   protect American business interests

   2   improve social and economic conditions

   3   abolish slavery in the South

   4   settle the American frontier

5   **Elizabeth Cady Stanton, Susan B. Anthony, and Lucretia Mott are best remembered for their efforts to**

   1   organize labor unions

   2   expose government corruption

   3   obtain the vote for women

   4   limit immigration

6   **Information about the rebellion in Cuba, the sinking of the battleship *Maine*, and "yellow journalism" would be found in a textbook chapter on the**

   1   Spanish-American War

   2   Boxer Rebellion

   3   Progressive Movement

   4   World War I

Base your answer to question 7 on the cartoon below.

The Spanish Brute

Library of Congress

7   **What is the main idea of the cartoon?**

   1   Nations will fight only when attacked.

   2   Government policies in a democracy are often brutal.

   3   Spain's brutality led to the Spanish-American War.

   4   Cubans were the cause of the explosion of the battleship *Maine*.

8   **Which headline best reflects the idea of imperialism?**

   1   "Supreme Court Bans School Segregation"

   2   "President Roosevelt Meets with Russian Leaders"

   3   "The United States to Buy Japanese Cars"

   4   "President McKinley Announces U.S. Occupation of the Philippines"

9 **A major goal of the United States during World War I was to**
   1 end the spread of Communism   **3** defend freedom of the seas
   2 take over Latin America   **4** eliminate the need for allies

Base your answer to question 10 on the following cartoon.

10 **The situation in the cartoon best illustrates which U.S. policy?**
   1 Monroe Doctrine
   2 Open Door Policy
   3 "Big Stick Policy"
   4 neutrality

President Theodore Roosevelt as the World Constable

11 **What was the main reason for creating the League of Nations?**
   1 to regulate international trade   **3** to organize future Olympics
   2 to preserve world peace   **4** to punish the German nation

12 **Women's status changed as a result of World War I mainly because**
   1 large numbers of women served in the armed forces
   2 many women were sent to relocation centers
   3 greater job opportunities became available to women
   4 women were accepted into elementary schools for the first time

13 **A large number of business failures, high rates of unemployment, and falling production are characteristics of a period of**
   1 depression   **3** expansion
   2 prosperity   **4** recovery

14 **A major result of the New Deal was that it**
   1 guaranteed health care to senior citizens
   2 extended the merit system in the civil service
   3 destroyed the free enterprise system
   4 expanded the role of the federal government

Base your answer to question 15 on the graph.

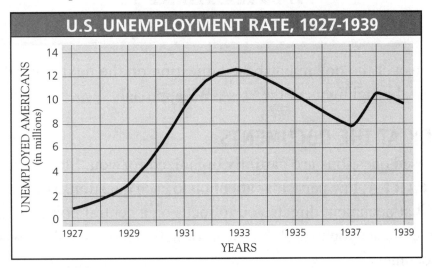

15 **According to the graph, what happened to the unemployment rate between 1933 and 1937?**

   1 It gradually decreased.   **3** It decreased rapidly.

   2 It gradually increased.   **4** It remained the same.

CONSTRUCTED-RESPONSE QUESTION

Base your answers to questions 1 through 3 on the timeline below and your knowledge of social studies.

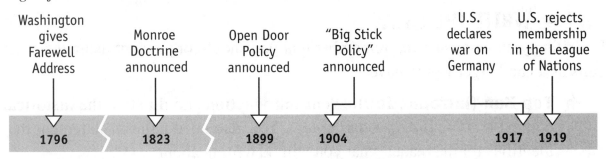

1. Which foreign policy decision involved events in Asia? _____

2. Which item on the timeline came first: the Monroe Doctrine or the "Big Stick Policy"? _____

3. Select one decision on the timeline, and explain why it was made. _____

_____

ANSWERING A DOCUMENT-BASED QUESTION

Before you answer the document-based question on the next several pages, let's quickly review the highlights of the "L•A•W" approach.

"L"— LOOK AT THE DOCUMENTS

Document-based questions are partially organized for you. Start by answering the questions in **PART A.** Pay particular attention to each question. Think about how the question for that document directs you to focus on a central point of the document. The question will lead you to look for the information the testmakers want you to get out of that document.

"A" — ANALYZE THE DOCUMENTS

Use the information you provided in the answers to the questions following each document to write your essay. To help you organize this information, create a **Document Box.** Remember that fully answering the questions in **PART A** and using that information in **PART B** will *not* be enough to gain full credit on your answer. Another important requirement of the *Task* is that you provide additional information from your knowledge of social studies. This information can be added to the bottom of your **Document Box.**

"W" — WRITE THE ESSAY

In writing your essay answer, remember that you should organize it using the same parts as a hamburger would have:

★ **Top Bun (Introduction).** Your introduction should state the historical context (*setting the time and place*). You also need a thesis statement that identifies for the reader what you will be writing about.

★ **Patties of Meat (Supporting Paragraphs).** These paragraphs use evidence from the documents to answer the *Task* questions. Each paragraph should be directed toward answering one of the *Task* questions. Use your **Document Box** to see where to locate supporting information.

★ **Bottom Bun (Conclusion).** The last paragraph should restate the historical context and summarize the most important evidence or ideas you have provided in support of your thesis statement.

This question is based on the accompanying documents (1-6). The question is designed to test your ability to work with historical documents. Some of the documents have been edited for the purpose of the question. As you analyze the documents, take into account both the context of each document and any point of view that may be presented in the document.

Historical Context:

> The decision to go to war is one of the most serious choices made by any nation. Throughout their history, Americans have made this choice for a variety of reasons.

Task:

> Using information from at least 4 documents and your knowledge of social studies, answer the questions that follow each document in Part A. Your answers to the questions will help you write the Part B essay in which you will be asked to
>
> Select **two** of the wars dealt with in the documents. For each war you select:
>
> - *Identify* the war.
> - *Explain* **one** reason why Americans became involved in that war.
> - *Discuss* **one** result of that war.

PART A: SHORT ANSWER

Directions: Analyze the documents and answer the short-answer questions that follow each document in the space provided.

DOCUMENT 1

> "Whenever any form of government becomes destructive of [the people's rights], it is the right of the people to alter or abolish it … The history of the present King of Britain is the history of repeated injuries … all having in direct object the establishment of an absolute tyranny over these states."
>
> — *Declaration of Independence, July 4, 1776*

1. According to the Declaration, why did the American colonists go to war with

Great Britain? _____ **[1]**

DOCUMENT 2

"We, the people of the United States, in order to form a more perfect Union, establish justice, insure [peace], provide for the common defense, promote the general welfare, and secure the blessings of liberty to ourselves and our [children], do ordain and establish this Constitution for the United States of America."

— *Preamble (introduction) to the U.S. Constitution*

2. According to the Preamble, what task faced Americans after their victory over

   Britain? _____ [1]

DOCUMENT 3

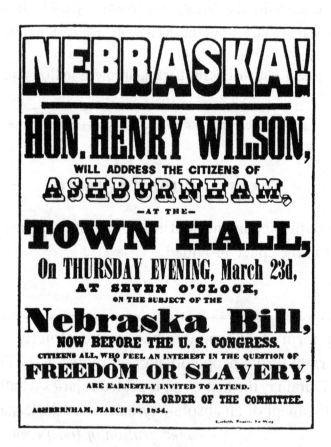

3a. What was the issue that Congressman Wilson would address? _____

_____ [1]

3b. How did this issue eventually lead to the outbreak of the Civil War? _____

_____ [2]

DOCUMENT 4

> Neither slavery nor involuntary servitude, except as a punishment for crimes …, shall exist within the United States, or any place subject to their [laws].
> — *Thirteenth Amendment, December 6, 1865*

4. What change did this amendment bring about just after the Civil War?

_____ **[2]**

DOCUMENT 5

The New York Times

VOL. LXIV	NEW YORK, SATURDAY, MAY 8, 1915	One Cent

LUSITANIA SUNK BY GERMAN SUBMARINE
Twice Torpedoed Off Irish Coast

Probably 1,260 Dead, 128 Are Americans; Washington Sees a Crisis at Hand

5a. How many Americans were killed when the British passenger ship *Lusitania* was attacked by a German submarine? _____ **[1]**

5b. How did this incident affect American attitudes toward Germany? _____

_____ **[2]**

DOCUMENT 6

> ### MINUTES OF THE U.S. SENATE (NOVEMBER, 1919)
>
> "What is the result of this Treaty of Versailles? We have entangled ourselves with all European concerns. We are asked to join in alliance with the European nations which have joined the League of Nations. We will surrender once and for all our great policy of 'no entangling alliances' upon which the strength of this Republic has been based for 150 years. I suggest we return to this policy and reject involvement in the League of Nations."
>
> — *Senator William Borah, addressing the Senate*

6. What foreign policy did Senator Borah recommend to Americans at the end of World War I? _____ [1]

PART B: ESSAY

Directions: Write a well-organized essay that includes an introduction, several paragraphs, and a conclusion. Use evidence from at least **three** documents in the body of your essay. Support your response with specfic relevant facts, examples, and details. Include additional outside information.

Historical Context:

> The decision to go to war is one of the most serious choices made by any nation. Throughout their history, Americans have made this choice for a variety of reasons.

Task:

> Using information from the documents and your knowledge of social studies, write an essay in which you
>
> Select **two** of the wars dealt with in the documents. For each war you select:
>
> - *Identify* the war.
> - *Explain* **one** reason why Americans became involved in that war.
> - *Discuss* **one** result of that war.

CHAPTER 10

THE UNITED STATES AS A WORLD LEADER, From 1941 to Present

In this chapter, you will learn how American attempts to avoid a foreign war failed, when Japan attacked Pearl Harbor. After World War II, the U.S. and Soviet Union emerged as superpowers. The 1950s and 1960s were a time of social reform. This reform period ended with the Vietnam War. In the 1970s, the nation sank into a recession. In the 1980s and 1990s, Americans recovered and took on a new world role.

National Archives

World War II marked a major turning point in U.S. history

★ **World War II and the Cold War.** During World War II, Americans helped defeat German and Japanese aggression. After the war, America and the Soviet Union became rivals in the "Cold War."

★ **Civil Rights and Reform, 1950–1968.** The Supreme Court ended racial segregation in public schools. President Johnson introduced "Great Society" programs to help the poor. Women demanded greater equality.

★ **From Crisis to Prosperity, 1968–present.** Failure in Vietnam and the Watergate scandal weakened the Presidency. President Reagan restored prosperity. President Bush witnessed the end of the Cold War. Under President Clinton, Americans enjoyed an economic boom.

In studying this period, you should focus on the following questions:

★ What were the causes of World War II and the Cold War?

★ What key social developments occurred in the 1950s and 1960s?

★ How did the Vietnam War and the Watergate Scandal affect Americans?

MAJOR THEMES IN U.S. HISTORY: CONTRIBUTIONS OF INDIVIDUALS

Throughout American history, some individuals have made decisions or performed acts that have had important effects on the lives of others. Five types of individuals have had a special impact on other Americans: our Presidents, social reformers, business leaders, inventors, and authors.

PRESIDENTS OF THE UNITED STATES

The President is not only the chief executive of our federal government, but symbolizes our nation to the world. The President has charge of our foreign policy, military preparedness, and national economic policy. Today, the President can communicate to millions of Americans simply by appearing on television. In preparing for the test, familiarize yourself with the Presidents who have most influenced the course of American history. These Presidents include:

★ George Washington   ★ Woodrow Wilson
★ Thomas Jefferson   ★ Franklin D. Roosevelt
★ Andrew Jackson   ★ John F. Kennedy
★ Abraham Lincoln   ★ Lyndon B. Johnson
★ Theodore Roosevelt   ★ Richard Nixon

SOCIAL REFORMERS

Unlike the President, social reformers do not hold political office and do not have the powers of the U.S. government behind them. Instead, they share an ability to manage and mobilize people. These reformers have a vision for the future, an ability to communicate it to others, and the power to motivate others to act. Great reformers, like Martin Luther King, Jr., have been able to organize people into powerful groups that pushed for major changes in society. Some of the more important include:

★ Elizabeth Cady Stanton   ★ Samuel Gompers
★ Susan B. Anthony   ★ Martin Luther King, Jr.

BUSINESS LEADERS AND INVENTORS

Great leaders of business are able to organize people and direct their activities towards the production of goods and services in the most efficient way possible. Inventors show us new ways to produce goods and services. Some of the most important business leaders and inventors include:

★ Samuel Slater

★ Robert Fulton

★ Alexander Graham Bell

★ Andrew Carnegie

★ John D. Rockefeller

★ Thomas Edison

★ Henry Ford

★ Bill Gates

AUTHORS

New ideas, when they are powerfully expressed, can have a major impact on the course of a nation's history. Some writers who have greatly influenced our nation's history include the following:

AUTHOR	MAJOR WORK	IMPACT
Thomas Paine (1776)	In *Common Sense*, Paine urged colonists to break away from Great Britain. He ridiculed the idea of an island ruling a continent.	This pamphlet helped convince colonists to revolt against Britain and to fight for independence.
Alexander Hamilton (1787)	Madison, Jay, and Hamilton wrote *The Federalist*, explaining why the new Constitution should be adopted.	This group of essays helped persuade Americans to ratify the new U.S. Constitution.
Harriet Beecher Stowe (1852)	In *Uncle Tom's Cabin*, Stowe described the horrors of slavery as they existed in the deep South.	The book stirred Northern sentiment to end slavery. It gave increased vigor to the abolitionist cause.
Upton Sinclair (1906)	Sinclair's novel *The Jungle* described the unsanitary conditions in the meat-packing industry.	The book shocked the nation, prompting legislation that regulated the food and drug industries.
Rachel Carson (1962)	In her book, *Silent Spring*, Carson warned Americans about the harmful effects of insecticides and pesticides.	The book led to a greater awareness of the need to protect the environment and safeguard against insecticides.

MAJOR HISTORICAL DEVELOPMENTS

WORLD WAR II AND THE COLD WAR

WORLD WAR II: 1941–1945

The Great Depression spread from the United States to Europe, where it led to the rise of dictators like **Adolf Hitler** in Germany. Hitler allied with the dictator **Benito Mussolini** in Italy and the military government of Japan. World War II began in Europe in 1939 when Germany invaded Poland.

THE UNITED STATES ENTERS WORLD WAR II, 1941

To avoid involvement in future wars, Congress had passed the **Neutrality Acts** (1937–1939), prohibiting Americans from selling arms to warring nations. Nevertheless, President Roosevelt pushed through **Lend-Lease** and other laws allowing Americans to send supplies to the British. Surprisingly, events in Asia, not Europe, brought the United States into the war. Japanese planes launched a surprise attack on the U.S. fleet stationed at **Pearl Harbor,** Hawaii. The next day, President Roosevelt asked Congress to declare war on Japan. Germany then declared war on the U.S.

The U.S.S. Shaw exploding during the surprise attack on Pearl Harbor

THE HOME FRONT

In order to fight the war, industries quickly changed from producing consumer goods to wartime materials. As factory workers entered the armed services, many women and African Americans took their places. One side effect of the war was the forced relocation of Japanese Americans from the West Coast. President Roosevelt ordered their removal to inland internment centers to prevent spying or sabotage. The Supreme Court upheld the relocations as a military necessity in *Korematsu v. United States* **(1944).** Recently, Congress apologized for this act.

THE WAR AGAINST GERMANY

By the time America entered the war, Hitler had conquered most of Europe. Hitler began exterminating Jews, gypsies, the disabled and the mentally ill in what has become known as the **Holocaust.** Twelve million people were killed in concentration camps. The **Allies** (*Britain, the United States, and the Soviet Union*) decided to focus on defeating Germany first. After defeating German forces in North Africa, the Allies landed in Italy. Finally, in mid-1944, U.S. and British troops invaded Germany from the west, while the Soviets attacked from the east. In May 1945, Germany surrendered.

THE WAR AGAINST JAPAN

Once Germany was defeated, Americans began preparations for an invasion of Japan. To avoid millions of casualties, President Truman decided to use a new weapon, the atomic bomb, against Japan. Truman selected **Hiroshima** and **Nagasaki** as targets. Nearly 130,000 people were killed in these two cities. Japan surrendered in August 1945, just after these attacks.

General Douglas MacArthur (at microphone) accepts Japan's surrender aboard the U.S.S. Missouri

THE LEGACY OF WORLD WAR II

World War II was a global disaster. Fifty million people had been killed, while much of Europe, Africa and Asia lay in ruins.

THE TREATMENT OF GERMANY, 1945–1946

The Allies put leading Nazis on trial in Nuremberg, Germany. In these **Nuremburg Trials,** most of these leaders were found guilty of atrocities and hanged. This showed the world that individuals were responsible for their actions, even in times of war, and would be held to certain universal standards. Germany was then divided into four occupation zones and occupied by the armies of the United States, Great Britain, France, and the Soviet Union.

THE OCCUPATION OF JAPAN

U.S. forces also occupied Japan. **Douglas MacArthur** was assigned the job of reforming the Japanese government and society. Japan was forbidden from having a large army or navy, and renounced the use of nuclear weapons and waging war. A new constitution went into effect in 1947, making Japan a democracy.

General Douglas MacArthur

Library of Congress

THE RISE OF THE SUPERPOWERS

The collapse of European power left the United States and Soviet Union as the world's two **superpowers.** The United States had tremendous economic power and the atomic bomb. The Soviets had the world's largest army, which occupied most of Eastern Europe.

THE END OF EUROPEAN IMPERIALISM

The struggle for democracy against dictatorship and the collapse of European power led colonies in Asia and Africa to seek their independence.

THE NEW YORK CONNECTION

Throughout the war, the allies had discussed how to keep the peace after the war. Despite the failure of the League of Nations, the allies decided to form a new international peace-keeping organization: the **United Nations.** According to the United Nations Charter, the aim of the organization was to maintain world peace, while trying to foster friendship and cooperation among nations. The U.N., headquartered in New York City, also seeks to eliminate hunger, disease and ignorance around the world.

The United Nations in New York City

United Nations, 177477/S. Lwin

THE COLD WAR

After Germany surrendered, serious differences arose between the United States and Soviet Union over the future of Eastern Europe. Soon they became rivals in a **Cold War** —which was "cold" only in the sense that the two superpowers never fought one another directly in open warfare.

SOVIET SATELLITES, 1946

ROOTS OF THE COLD WAR

The roots of the Cold War lay in the differences between the democratic, capitalist system of the United States and the Communist system of the Soviet Union. The Soviets had occupied Eastern Europe while fighting Germany. When the war ended, Soviet leader **Joseph Stalin** pledged to withdraw Soviet troops and to hold free elections. Instead, Stalin placed Communist "puppet" governments in power throughout Eastern Europe. Trade between Eastern and Western Europe was cut off. It seemed as if an **"Iron Curtain"** had fallen, closing off Eastern Europe from the West.

CONTAINMENT IN EUROPE

American leaders responded by developing the policy of **containment** — acting to prevent the spread of Communism to new countries, while accepting Communist governments where they were already established.

★ **The Truman Doctrine, 1947.** When Communists threatened Greece and Turkey, President Truman gave these countries military aid. This prompted Truman to promise U.S. support to any nation fighting Communism.

★ **The Marshall Plan, 1948.** Truman's Secretary of State, George Marshall, proposed a program of economic aid to Western European countries to help them rebuild and to better resist Communism. The **Marshall Plan** successfully speeded up the economic recovery of Western Europe.

★ **The Division of Germany and the Berlin Airlift.** In 1948, the French, British and Americans united their occupation zones into a single West German state. The old German capital, Berlin, was located within the Russian zone, but had also been divided into four occupation sectors. Stalin reacted to the merging of the Western zones of Germany by closing all highway and railroad links to West Berlin. The Western Allies began a massive airlift to supply the city. After 11 months, Stalin lifted the blockade.

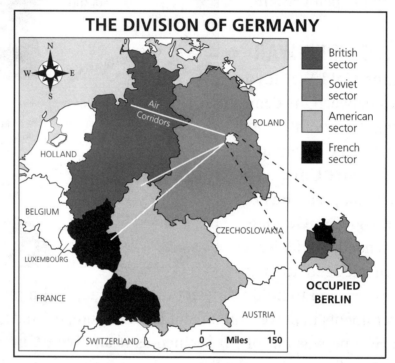

★ **The Formation of NATO.** In 1949, the U.S., and ten Western European countries formed **NATO** (*North Atlantic Treaty Organization*) to protect Western Europe from a Communist invasion. The Soviets responded by creating the **Warsaw Pact.**

THE POLICY OF CONTAINMENT IN ASIA

Just when Americans believed they had checked the spread of Communism in Europe, the world's most populated nation, China, became Communist.

★ **The Fall of China, 1949.** Since the 1920s, Communists had been trying to overthrow the Nationalist government of China. After World War II, fighting between the Nationalists and the Communists grew fiercer. The Communists, led by **Mao Zedong,** finally defeated the Nationalist government in 1949. Mao and his followers established Communism in China.

★ **The Korean War, 1950–1953.** After World War II, Korea was divided into a northern and southern part. In the northern part, a Communist government was established, while a non-Communist government took over the South. In 1950, North Korea invaded South Korea in an attempt to unify the country under Communist rule. With U.N. approval, President Truman ordered U.S. forces into South Korea

U.S. soldiers on the move as they cross the Naktong River in Korea (1950)

to resist the invasion. In 1951, U.S. forces entered North Korea and advanced to the Chinese border. China entered the war in support of its ally, North Korea. Truman rejected General MacArthur's recommendation to use nuclear weapons. Fighting ended when a peace agreement was signed in 1953, leaving Korea divided exactly as it had been before the war.

THE EFFECT OF THE COLD WAR ON U.S. SECURITY

Americans became concerned about the possibility of a Communist threat within the United States. Many people were accused of "un-American" acts, and some even lost their jobs. In 1950, Senator **Joseph McCarthy** claimed he knew the names of hundreds of Communists working in the American government. Although McCarthy never proved his claims, he frightened many people. The term **"McCarthyism"** has come to mean making charges about a person's loyalty without offering any evidence.

Senator Joseph McCarthy

By 1949, the Soviets possessed atomic weapons. In 1957, the Soviet Union launched **Sputnik,** the first man-made satellite, into space. With missiles that could travel into space, the Soviet Union now had the ability to fire nuclear weapons at the United States.

THE COLD WAR IN LATIN AMERICA

In 1959, **Fidel Castro** established a Communist government in Cuba. American leaders feared that Communism might spread throughout Latin America. In 1961, anti-Castro Cubans trained in the United States invaded Cuba in an attempt to overthrow Castro. When the new President, **John F. Kennedy,** refused to supply the invading rebels with air support, the rebels were defeated. This was a major foreign policy failure for the Kennedy Administration.

Fidel Castro (seated)
before seizing power in Cuba

The Cuban Missile Crisis. Kennedy had a chance to regain his prestige in another confrontation with Cuba. In October 1962, spy planes discovered the Soviets were secretly building bases in Cuba with nuclear missiles aimed at the United States. Kennedy ordered U.S. forces on full alert. U.S. bombers and missiles were armed with nuclear weapons. Kennedy then imposed a blockade around Cuba. Both sides threatened each other with nuclear war, but Soviet leader **Nikita Khrushchev** withdrew the missiles in exchange for a promise by Kennedy never to invade Cuba.

THE CUBAN MISSILE CRISIS: 1962

ATLANTIC OCEAN

Wash. D.C. - 1130 miles
New York - 1300 miles
Chicago - 1310 miles
New Orleans - 650 miles

Gulf of Mexico

Havana
BAHAMAS
CUBA

MEXICO

JAMAICA

HAITI   DOMINICAN   PUERTO
         REPUBLIC   RICO

Missile Site
Zone of U.S. naval blockade
Range of targeted U.S. cities

0   Miles   500

THE WAR IN VIETNAM

The Cold War next spread to Southeast Asia. Vietnam had been a French colony since the 1800s. Vietnamese nationalists, fighting for independence, defeated the French in 1954. At the peace conference, Vietnam was divided in two. Vietnamese Communists received control of the north. A non-Communist state was created in the south. Vietnam was to be reunited after free elections. When the elections were not held, South Vietnamese Communists, known as **Vietcong,** launched a guerrilla war with North Vietnamese support to reunite the country under Communist rule.

★ **The War under President Kennedy.** President Kennedy and many other Americans believed if South Vietnam fell to Communism, other Asian nations would follow. He sent military advisors to help defend South Vietnam, hoping it would develop into a democratic nation.

★ **The War under President Johnson.** A major turning point occurred in 1964, when Congress gave President Johnson authority to halt North Vietnamese aggression. Over the next three years, Johnson sent large numbers of U.S. troops to Vietnam. In 1968, the Vietcong and the North Vietnamese launched attacks throughout South Vietnam, showing the Americans they were far from winning the war. Back home, anti-war protests grew in force.

President Lyndon Johnson visits American soldiers on a trip to Vietnam during in 1966

★ **The War under President Nixon.** Richard Nixon campaigned for the Presidency in 1968, promising to bring "peace with honor" in Vietnam. However, the war dragged on for five more years. Frustrated by attempts to end the war, Nixon began gradually withdrawing U.S. forces. In 1973, Nixon's representatives worked out an agreement with the North Vietnamese, known as the **Paris Peace Accords.** Under its terms, America withdrew from South Vietnam. Two years later, the Communists took over South Vietnam.

PROSPERITY AND CIVIL RIGHTS, 1950–1968

Production refers to the making of goods and services, while **consumption** refers to the use of these products by consumers and businesses. During the 1950s and 1960s, new patterns of production and consumption resulted in economic expansion.

POSTWAR PROSPERITY AND OPTIMISM

The United States became the largest producer of goods and services after World War II. Improving technology increased worker productivity, as industries became increasingly automated. The demand for new goods like automobiles, television sets and refrigerators constantly grew. A large

Automobile production was greatly aided by advances in automation and technology

number of children were born in the late 1940s and 1950s in a postwar "**baby boom**," creating a demand for housing, education, and related services. More women entered the workforce. A greater number of Americans became employed in service jobs such as teaching, health care, and banking. Despite the prosperity of the two decades following World War II, there were significant pockets of poverty — especially in rural areas and among some minority groups.

THE CIVIL RIGHTS MOVEMENT

The **Civil Rights Movement** was a major turning point in American history. It placed a greater focus on the goals of equality and democracy.

BROWN v. BOARD OF EDUCATION, 1954

After Reconstruction, Southern states passed Jim Crow laws which imposed racial segregation and took away voting rights from African Americans. In ***Plessy v. Ferguson*** (1896), the U.S. Supreme Court upheld the constitutionality of "separate but equal" facilities for blacks and whites supporting racially segregated facilities. In 1953, the N.A.A.C.P. filed a case on behalf of an African-American student denied admission to a white public school near her home. The N.A.A.C.P. argued the education of black students was inferior — since it implied they were not good enough to be educated with white students. In ***Brown v. Board of Education,*** the Supreme Court ruled that segregation in public schools was unconstitutional, ending racial segregation in public schools.

THE LEADERSHIP OF DR. MARTIN LUTHER KING, JR.

Dr. Martin Luther King, Jr. became the leader of the Civil Rights Movement in the mid-1950s. King believed the best way to change the attitudes of racists was through non-violent protest. King carried out his resistance through **civil disobedience.** One of the most successful campaigns was the **Montgomery Bus Boycott** (1955), sparked by **Rosa Parks.** Parks refused to sit in the back

Martin Luther King, Jr. leads the March on Washington

of a segregated bus. African Americans boycotted the buses and carpooled to work. Dr. King was brought in to lead the campaign. The boycott successfully ended racial segregation on public buses in Montgomery, Alabama.

King and others continued to oppose racial segregation with boycotts, picketing, and sit-ins. King often faced violence from those who opposed him. In 1963, King delivered his **"I Have a Dream" Speech** at the Lincoln Memorial as part of the **March on Washington.** The speech focused the nation's attention on the problems faced by African Americans deprived of their civil rights. In 1964, Congress passed the **Civil Rights Act,** prohibiting discrimination on the basis of race or religion in businesses involved in interstate commerce. In 1965, Congress passed the **Voting Rights Act,** prohibiting practices that were being used to prevent African Americans from voting.

OTHER GROUPS FOLLOW THE AFRICAN-AMERICAN LEAD

Following the success of the Civil Rights Movement, women, Native American Indians, the disabled and other groups sought greater equality in society. The Supreme Court, led by Chief Justice **Earl Warren,** also moved to protect individual rights, including the rights of the accused. For example, in *Miranda v. Arizona* (1966), the Court ruled that police could not interrogate an accused person without first telling the person of his or her right to have a lawyer present or to remain silent.

Presidents **John F. Kennedy** (1961–1963) and **Lyndon B. Johnson** (1963–1968) also attempted to promote social reform. They proposed civil rights legislation and programs to improve education and reduce poverty. President Johnson introduced his **"Great Society"** programs, which included Medicare, aid to education, and assistance to inner cities and rural districts. Johnson's **affirmative action** programs promoted the hiring of minorities and women.

THE WOMEN'S LIBERATION MOVEMENT

Although they achieved the right to vote in 1920, women continued to make only gradual progress towards achieving equality. By the 1960s, many American women wanted equal pay for equal work. Influenced in part by the success of the Civil Rights Movement, they wanted careers and the ability to earn as much as men did. The **Women's Liberation Movement** achieved important gains for women, both in the workplace and in society at large.

Education. New programs promoted hiring women professors. More women were admitted into military academies, law schools, and medical schools.

Employment. Federal aid was provided to build child-care centers. Laws were passed requiring companies to pay women the same wages for the same work.

IMPACT OF THE WOMEN'S LIBERATION MOVEMENT

Other Changes. More funds were spent for research on women's diseases. As women assumed greater responsibilities in the workplace, they urged men to share domestic duties like cooking and cleaning. Many women adopted "Ms." instead of "Miss" or "Mrs."

FROM CRISIS TO PROSPERITY, 1968–PRESENT

In the last thirty years, Americans have moved from a crisis of confidence in the late 1960s and early 1970s to new levels of peace and prosperity.

THE CRISIS OF CONFIDENCE

In the later 1960s, Americans entered a period of crisis. At home, Americans were shaken by the assassination of a number of important leaders — President John F. Kennedy (1963), Dr. Martin Luther King, Jr. (1968), and Robert F. Kennedy (1969).

INCREASING MILITANCY

Although the Civil Rights Movement made great strides in ending racial segregation, many African Americans still faced prejudice and discrimination. Some African Americans became militant, believing equality could only be obtained through violence. When Dr. King was assassinated in 1968, rioting erupted in many cities across the nation. Other minority groups mirrored the mili-

Antiwar discontent grows as young people burn their draft cards to protest the Vietnam War

tancy of African Americans. These minority groups also took new and more forceful steps to obtain national attention. Members of the **American Indian Movement** (AIM) seized Alcatraz Island in San Francisco and the monument at Wounded Knee, South Dakota. Tensions further escalated with the Vietnam War. Youths burned their draft cards, and students across the nation joined in mass protests and demonstrations, closing hundreds of college campuses in 1969.

THE WATERGATE CRISIS

The American failure in Vietnam made many Americans lose confidence in their national leaders. Congress passed the **War Powers Act** (1973), requiring the President to seek Congressional approval soon after sending troops overseas. Confidence was further strained by the **Watergate Crisis.**

Nixon delivers his inaugural address, January 20, 1969

In 1972, a group working for Nixon's re-election was caught breaking into the Democratic Party headquarters at the Watergate building in Washington, D.C. President Nixon and his advisers tried to cover up the investigation. During the investigation, it was revealed that Nixon had secretly taped his White House conversations. Nixon refused to turn over the tapes. The Supreme Court ordered him to turn the tapes over, however, supporting the principle that not even a President is above the law. The tapes showed that Nixon had lied when he said he was not involved in the cover-up. Threatened with impeachment, Nixon resigned the Presidency.

STAGFLATION AND OTHER TROUBLES

Nixon and later Presidents also had to deal with soaring **inflation** (*rising prices*). This was made worse when countries exporting oil limited their production, raising world oil prices. The result was severe inflation and high unemployment in the early 1970s, known as **stagflation.** Presidents Ford and Carter tried to curb stagflation without much success. President Carter also faced troubles in Iran. In 1978, demonstrations overthrew the Shah of Iran and put a Muslim religious leader in his place. Iranians seized the U.S. Embassy in Iran and held 50 staff members hostage for more than a year. President Carter seemed powerless to free the hostages, and lost the election of 1980 to **Ronald Reagan.**

A RECOVERY OF CONFIDENCE

President Reagan reversed the trend of ever-increasing federal power begun during the New Deal. Reagan cut federal programs, eliminated many regulations on business, and cut federal taxes. Reagan also increased military spending, which he paid for by increasing the **federal deficit** — what the government pays for by borrowing. These policies spurred the economy. However, his programs greatly increased the **national debt.**

In foreign policy, Reagan announced that the United States would take steps to "roll back" Communism. Reagan sent aid to rebels fighting Communist governments in Afghanistan and other places. When Congress prohibited Reagan from aiding anti-Communist rebels in Nicaragua, several high officials in his administration secretly used funds from arms sales to Iran to aid these Nicaraguan rebels. Revelation of their actions led to the **Iran-Contra Scandal.** An investigation into the scandal cleared Reagan himself of wrongdoing.

THE END OF THE COLD WAR

Because the Soviet economy under Communism was failing, Soviet leader **Mikhail Gorbachev** introduced greater openness and freedom into Soviet society. This eventually led to the collapse of Communism in the Soviet Union and independence for the nations of Eastern Europe. In 1989, the Berlin Wall was torn down and Germany was reunited. In 1991, the Soviet Union itself split apart.

THE UNITED STATES SEEKS A NEW WORLD ROLE

Even before the collapse of the Soviet Union, American leaders had been searching for a new role in world affairs. In 1977, President Carter signed the **Panama Canal Treaty,** which eventually gave the canal to Panama in 1999. Carter also promoted peace in the Middle East. Egypt and Israel had frequently been at war. Carter invited leaders from both countries to Camp David, Maryland in 1977. In the **Camp David Accords,** Egypt and Israel agreed to a peace settlement.

Sadat was assassinated by Arabs who felt he had "sold out" to Israel

When the Cold War finally ended in 1989, **President George Bush** called for Americans to participate in a "New World Order." To protect world oil supplies, Bush sent U.S. forces to drive Iraqi troops out of Kuwait during the **Persian Gulf War.** The U.S. was joined by a coalition of other nations. The war freed Kuwait and protected world oil supplies. Bush also

A U.S. soldier atop a captured Iraqi tank as oil wells burn in the background

sent troops to Somalia in Africa, where they helped protect emergency food supplies from conflicts by local warlords.

THE CLINTON PRESIDENCY

President Clinton takes the oath of office

Bush's successor, **President Bill Clinton,** continued to promote America's new role as a world peacekeeper. Clinton intervened in Eastern Europe to stop the violence in Bosnia and Kosovo, which had become battlegrounds between racial and ethnic groups. President Clinton also promoted hemispheric cooperation by supporting **NAFTA** — the **North American Free Trade Agreement.** Under NAFTA, tariffs between Mexico, Canada, and the U.S. are gradually being reduced. Canada already enjoys free trade with the United States. President Clinton further encouraged the peace process in the Middle East by promoting talks between Israel, its Arab neighbors, and the **P.L.O.,** a group representing the Palestinian Arabs.

President Clinton presided over a booming economy. Advances in computer technology brought business profits to all-time highs. Nevertheless, Clinton faced scandal when he was accused of lying under oath about his personal affairs. He became only the second President to be impeached by the House of Representatives. However, the Senate failed to convict him of the charges and he completed his second term.

THE ELECTION OF 2000

Our President is chosen by the Electoral College. When voters in a state vote for the President, they actually choose electors from their state. Each candidate usually wins all or none of the state's electoral votes. Because of this system, candidates spend more time in states with large numbers of electoral votes. Sometimes, because of the Electoral College, the winner of the popular vote does not win the election. This happened in 2000. **George W. Bush,** son of former President Bush, was elected President although his opponent, Clinton's Vice President **Al Gore,** won the popular vote. In some states the margin was so narrow that the winner of the electoral vote was at first unclear. Gore challenged the vote count in Florida, which would have changed the election, but the U.S. Supreme Court blocked a recount.

THE GEORGE W. BUSH PRESIDENCY

On **September 11, 2001, al-Qaeda** terrorists crashed airplanes into the Pentagon and World Trade Center, killing thousands of people. Bush immediately declared a "War on Terrorism." Federal agents replaced private security agents at U.S. airports, and the **Office of Homeland Security** was created. When the Taliban government of Afghanistan refused to hand over al-Qaeda's leader, **Osama bin Laden,** the U.S. invaded Afghanistan. This led to the overthrew of the Taliban and the destruction of terrorist bases there.

War in Iraq. Bush and other world leaders also insisted that **Saddam Hussein** of Iraq prove he had no weapons of mass destruction (**WMDs**), which he might supply to terrorists. Iraq repeatedly denied it had such weapons. France, Germany, and Russia recommended U.N. inspectors be given more time to search for these weapons, but in March 2003, President Bush gave Hussein 48 hours to resign and leave Iraq. When Hussein refused, the U.S., Great Britain, and their allies attacked and quickly destroyed Iraq's ability to wage war. U.S forces entered Baghdad in April, as Hussein's regime collapsed. Late in 2003, Hussein was captured. Despite these successes, Iraq's occupation has proved difficult, with frequent terrorist attacks on U.S. forces. Religious and ethnic rivalries divide the Iraqi people, although elections were held in 2005. Meanwhile, in the United States, President Bush went on to win a second term in the 2004 election against Democratic candidate John Kerry.

PROSPERITY AND NEW CHALLENGES

Since World War II, America has entered a global economy. Recent improvements in communications and technology have greatly increased the pace of globalization. Americans now sell more products abroad and use more foreign goods and services than ever before. As a result, Americans now enjoy greater comfort and prosperity than at any other time in their history.

At the same time, Americans face many challenges ahead. They must decide what services to pay for with tax monies, and how much they should be taxed. The computer and Internet are destroying old industries almost as fast as they are creating new ones. Americans face greater competition from countries in Europe, Asia, Latin America, and Africa. Americans have also to address other problems. How can we decrease violent crime and substance abuse? Can we limit pollution, conserve natural resources, and protect the environment? Can we promote equality while balancing national unity with growing cultural diversity?

SUMMARIZING YOUR UNDERSTANDING

OVERARCHING THEME

Since 1941, the United States has occupied a position of world leadership — with profound effects inside the United States as well as abroad.

KEY TERMS, CONCEPTS, AND PEOPLE

★ World War II

★ *Korematsu v. United States*

★ Cold War

★ Containment

★ Civil Rights Movement

★ Martin Luther King, Jr.

★ *Brown v. Board of Education*

★ Vietnam War

TESTING YOUR UNDERSTANDING

MULTIPLE-CHOICE QUESTIONS

1   Which event caused the United States to declare war in 1941?
1   Japan's surprise attack on Pearl Harbor
2   the aggressive actions of Germany
3   the sinking of the passenger ship *Lusitania*
4   German attacks on American merchant ships

2   Which group of United States residents suffered the greatest loss of constitutional rights during World War II?
1   Italian Americans
2   Japanese Americans
3   German Americans
4   African Americans

3   The bombing of Hiroshima and Nagasaki resulted in
1   the end of World War II
2   U.S. entry into World War I
3   the surrender of Germany
4   the end of the Cold War

Base your answer to question 4 on the map below.

4   According to the map, which territories were controlled by Japan in World War II?

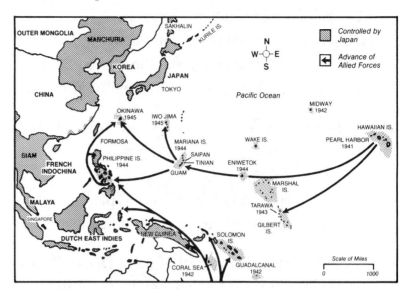

1   Manchuria and China

2   French Indochina and China

3   Outer Mongolia and Korea

4   Korea and Manchuria

5   Which was a major result of World War II?

1   Great Britain and France helped to rebuild the Soviet Union.

2   The United Nations was formed.

3   Germany gained control of Eastern Europe.

4   Italy was divided into two countries.

6   The United States joined the United Nations after World War II to

1   limit the spread of Communism in Europe

2   improve the nation's social and economic conditions

3   help prevent future wars

4   seek allies against the Japanese government

7   The term "Cold War" refers to

1   U.S. neutrality before World War II

2   attempts to appease Hitler

3   disputes between the Soviet Union and China

4   hostility between the United States and Soviet Union

8   The Marshall Plan and NATO were similar in that both sought to

1   to increase American power in Latin America

2   punish Germany for starting World War II

3   stop the expansion of Communism in Europe

4   gain military control of European nations

9 **A major goal of the Civil Rights Movement in the 1950s was to**
1 gain voting rights for women
2 stop the spread of Communism
3 end racial segregation in the United States
4 discourage African Americans from traveling to Africa

10 ***Brown v. Board of Education* was important because it established**
1 greater rights for accused persons
2 the right of women to vote
3 the "separate but equal" principle
4 the illegality of segregated public schools

11 **Martin Luther King's "I Have a Dream" speech was important because it**
1 led to improved living standards for many immigrants
2 called for a violent revolution in America's cities
3 drew attention to the inequalities faced by African Americans
4 helped win voting rights for 18-year olds

12 **Which was a cause of American involvement in the Vietnam War?**
1 religious differences between North and South Vietnam
2 American fear of Communist expansion in Asia
3 the North Korean invasion of South Vietnam
4 the Soviet use of nuclear weapons in Vietnam

Base your answer to question 13 on the following timeline.

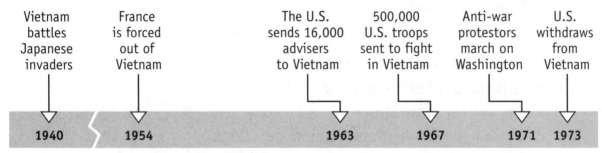

Vietnam battles Japanese invaders	France is forced out of Vietnam	The U.S. sends 16,000 advisers to Vietnam	500,000 U.S. troops sent to fight in Vietnam	Anti-war protestors march on Washington	U.S. withdraws from Vietnam
1940	1954	1963	1967	1971	1973

13 **The timeline indicates that the United States and Vietnam were**
1 involved in military conflict   3 sharing advanced technology
2 economic partners in Asia   4 allied against the French

Base your answer to question 14 on the graph below and your knowledge of social studies.

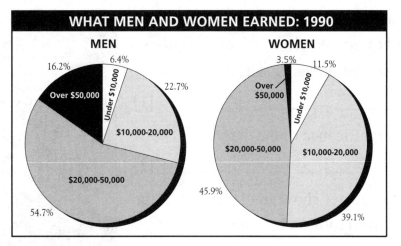

WHAT MEN AND WOMEN EARNED: 1990

14 **This graph deals with which major goal of the Women's Liberation Movement?**
1   to achieve the right to vote for American women
2   to decrease the number of women entering the workforce
3   to increase what male workers were paid
4   to gain equal pay for equal work

15 **An important result of the Watergate scandal was that it**
1   showed that even the President was not above the law
2   showed the ineffectiveness of the Supreme Court
3   displayed how ineffective Congress was in dealing with a crisis
4   indicated that the President has nearly unlimited powers

16 **In 1990, the United States government was concerned at Iraq's invasion of Kuwait in part because this region of the world**
1   supplies critical technology to the United States
2   is a major source of oil
3   provides most of the coal used in the United States
4   supplies wheat to the United States

17 **Under President Reagan, the budget deficit of the United States**
1   fell sharply   3   increased rapidly
2   remain unchanged   4   decreased slightly

CONSTRUCTED-RESPONSE QUESTION

Base your answers to questions 1 through 3 on the poster below and your knowledge of social studies.

...we here highly resolve that these dead shall not have died in vain...

REMEMBER DEC. 7th!

Source: *National Archives*

1. What is the source of this poster?

    **[1]**

2. What is the significance of the date

   December 7? _____ **[1]**

3. Why does the poster show smoke rising in the background and a torn American flag?

   _____

   _____ **[1]**

DOCUMENT-BASED QUESTION

This question is based on the accompanying documents (1-6). The question is designed to test your ability to work with historical documents. Some of the documents have been edited for the purpose of the question. As you analyze the documents, take into account both the source of each document and any point of view that may be presented in the document.

Historical Context:

> The ideas and actions of individuals often have a significant impact on others. One such individual, Dr. Martin Luther King, Jr., had an important impact on those around him and on future generations.

Task:

> Using information from the documents and your knowledge of social studies, answer the questions that follow each document in Part A. Your answers to the questions will help you write the Part B essay in which you will be asked to
>
> - *Identify* some of the injustices that were opposed by Dr. Martin Luther King.
> - *State* a belief that was part of Dr. Martin Luther King's philosophy.
> - *Discuss* **two** achievements of Dr. Martin Luther King that affected those around him and future generations.

PART A: SHORT ANSWER

Directions: Analyze the documents and answer the questions that follow each document in the space provided.

DOCUMENT 1

1. What does this photograph show about the treatment of African Americans in the South? _____

   _____

   _____

   _____ **[1]**

1940 water fountain, Mississippi

DOCUMENT 2

"Just last Thursday to be exact, one of the finest citizens in Montgomery [Alabama] was taken from a bus and carried to jail and arrested because she refused to get up to give her seat to a white person. Mrs. Rosa Parks is a fine person, and nobody can doubt the boundless outreach of her integrity. And just because she refused to get up, she was arrested."

— *Dr. Martin Luther King, speaking at a church in Montgomery, 1955*

2. Why was Rosa Parks arrested? _____ **[1]**

DOCUMENT 3

"I have been arrested [for] parading without a permit. Such a law becomes unjust when it is used to maintain segregation and to deny citizens [their rights]. In no sense do I advocate defying the law …. One who breaks an unjust law must do so openly, lovingly, and with a willingness to accept the penalty. An individual who breaks a law that conscience tells him is unjust, and accepts imprisonment to arouse the conscience of the community over its injustice, is expressing the highest respect for law."

— *Dr. Martin Luther King, Letter From Birmingham Jail, April 13, 1963*

3a. Why was Dr. King jailed? _____ **[1]**

3b. How did Dr. King feel about breaking laws? _____

_____ **[2]**

DOCUMENT 4

> "I say to you, my friends, that in spite of the difficulties and frustrations of the moment I still have a dream. …I have a dream that one day this nation will rise up and live out the true meaning of its creed (*beliefs*): "We hold these truths to be self-evident; that all men are created equal." I have a dream that one day in the red hills of Georgia the sons of former slaves and the sons of former slave owners will be able to sit down together at the table of brotherhood. … I have a dream that my four little children will one day live in a nation where they will not be judged by the color of their skin but by the content of their character. I have a dream today."
>
> — *"I Have a Dream" Speech by Dr. Martin Luther King, Washington, D.C.,1963*

4a. How did Dr. King believe his children were being judged in 1963? _____

_____ **[2]**

4b. What did Dr. King hope would happen in the future? _____

_____ **[2]**

DOCUMENT 5

The New York Times

| VOL.LXX | NEW YORK, FRIDAY JULY 2, 1964 | Ten Cents |

CIVIL RIGHTS ACT PASSED

Congress Moves to End
Racial and Religious Discrimination
President Johnson Signs Act the Same Day

5. Why is the Civil Rights Act seen as an achievement of Martin Luther King?

_____ **[2]**

DOCUMENT 6

**PERCENTAGE OF AFRICAN AMERICANS
REGISTERED TO VOTE IN THE SOUTH, 1960 AND 1966**

STATE	1960	1966	STATE	1960	1966
Texas	34.9%	58.5%	Georgia	29.3%	43.2%
Arkansas	37.6%	54.0%	Virginia	23.8%	44.0%
Louisiana	30.4%	42.3%	N. Carolina	31.3%	49.0%
Tennessee	58.9%	71.7%	S. Carolina	15.7%	45.1%
Mississippi	5.2%	27.8%	Florida	34.7%	62.1%
Alabama	15.2%	48.9%			

6. What trend occurred in registering of African-American voters in the South

between 1960 and 1966? _____

_____ **[2]**

PART B: ESSAY

Historical Context:

The ideas and actions of individuals often have a significant impact on others.
One such individual, Dr. Martin Luther King, Jr., had an important impact on those
around him and on future generations.

Task:

Using information from the documents and your knowledge of social studies, write
an essay in which you

- *Identify* some of the injustices that were opposed by Dr. Martin Luther King.
- *State* a belief that was part of Dr. Martin Luther King's philosophy.
- *Discuss* **two** achievements of Dr. Martin Luther King that affected those around
  him and future generations.

CHAPTER 11

A PRACTICE GRADE 8 INTERMEDIATE SOCIAL STUDIES TEST

Now that you have reviewed the material in this book, you should take a practice test to measure your progress. To help you, this chapter has a practice **Grade 8 Intermediate Social Studies Test.** However, before you begin, let's look at some common-sense tips for taking this test:

★ **Answer All the Questions.** Don't leave any questions unanswered. There is no penalty for guessing. Answer all questions, even if you're only guessing.

★ **Use the Process of Elimination.** When answering a multiple-choice question, it should be clear that certain choices are wrong. They are either irrelevant, lack a connection to the question, or are inaccurate statements. After you eliminate these choices, choose the best response that remains.

★ **Read the Question Carefully.** If a word in the question is unfamiliar, break it down into words that are familiar. Look at the prefix (start of the word), root, or suffix (ending) for clues to the meaning of the word.

Taking the examination that follows will help you to identify any areas in American history that you still need to study. Good luck on this practice test!

GRADE 8 SOCIAL STUDIES PRACTICE TEST

This practice test has three parts:

Part I has 1 45 multiple choice questions

Part II has 2 four constructed response questions

Part III has 3 one document-based essay

PART 1: ANSWER ALL QUESTIONS IN THIS PART

Directions: Each question is followed by four choices. Read each question carefully. Decide which choice is the correct answer and circle the number.

1 A study of the Maya, Incas, and Aztecs demonstrates that
   1   pre-Columbian peoples were largely uncivilized
   2   advanced American civilizations existed before Columbus arrived
   3   Europeans introduced agriculture to the Americas
   4   these people were peaceful prior to European conquest

2 Which would be a primary source about the lifestyle of the Algonquians?
   1   the remains of a wigwam
   2   a pueblo
   3   a book about the Native Americans of Long Island
   4   an article about totem poles

3 Which tribe is correctly paired with its geographical location?
   1   Seminoles — Northeast   3   Comanche — Northwest
   2   Apache — Southwest   4   Iroquois — Great Plains

4 The names New Amsterdam, New York, New France can best be used to show the
   1   influence of European nations in Colonial America
   2   British control of North America
   3   impact of Native American Indian cultures
   4   location of main cities at the time of the American Revolution

5 Colonial charters were most similar in purpose to present day
   1   constitutions   3   religions
   2   laws   4   settlements

6 Which feature of government was most fully developed during the colonial era?
   1   voting rights for women   3   representative assemblies
   2   equal rights for minorities   4   direct election of judges

Base your answer to question 8 on the circle graph below.

7   In 1775, which was the largest ethnic group in the colonies?

1   Scotch-Irish
2   German
3   English
4   African

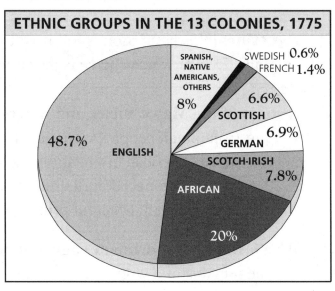

ETHNIC GROUPS IN THE 13 COLONIES, 1775

SPANISH, NATIVE AMERICANS, OTHERS 8%
SWEDISH 0.6%
FRENCH 1.4%
SCOTTISH 6.6%
GERMAN 6.9%
SCOTCH-IRISH 7.8%
ENGLISH 48.7%
AFRICAN 20%

8   Under the system of mercantilism, the British colonies provided Great Britain with

1   manufactured goods
2   raw materials and markets for British products
3   laborers for British factories
4   machinery and technological advice

Base your answer to question 9 on the poster to the right.

9   The "glorious news" announced in this document concerned which event in American history?

1   French and Indian War
2   American Revolution
3   Shays' Rebellion
4   Civil War

GLORIOUS NEWS.

PROVIDE̊CE, October 25, 1781.

Three o'Clock, P. M.

THIS MOMENT an EXPRESS arrived at his Honour the Deputy-Governor's, from Col. Chriſtopher Olney, Commandant on Rhode-Iſland, announcing the important Intelligence of the Surrender of Lord Cornwallis and his Army, an Account of which was printed This Morning at Newport, and is as follows, viz.

Newport, October 25, 1781.

YESTERDAY afternoon arrived in this Harbour Capt. Lovett, of the Schooner Adventure, from York-River, in Cheſapeak-Bay (which he left the 20th Inſtant) and brought us the glorious News of the Surrender of Lord CORNWALLIS and his Army Priſoners of War to the allied Army, under the Command of our illuſtrious General, and the French Fleet, under the Command of his Excellency the Count de GRASSE.

A Ceſſation of Arms took Place on Thurſday the 18th Inſtant, in Conſequence of Propoſals from Lord Cornwallis for a Capitulation. His Lordſhip propoſed a Ceſſation of Twenty-four Hours, but Two only were granted by His Excellency General WASHINGTON. The Articles were completed the ſame Day, and the next Day the allied Army took Poſſeſſion of York-Town.

By this glorious Conqueſt, NINE THOUSAND of the Enemy, including Seamen, fell into our Hands, with an immenſe Quantity of Warlike Stores, a forty Gun Ship, a Frigate, an armed Veſſel, and about One Hundred Sail of Tranſports.

Library of Congress

10   Which document has been accused of giving too little power to the central government?

1   Declaration of Independence
2   Articles of Confederation
3   United States Constitution
4   Magna Carta

11 **According to the United States Constitution, where does the power to govern come from?**

1 the President	**3** the people
2 acts of Congress	**4** Supreme Court decisions

12 **At the Constitutional Convention of 1787, differences involving representation were settled by creating a**

1 judicial system	**3** single President
2 two-house legislature	**4** a three branch government

Base your answer to question 13 on the timeline below.

13 **What would be the best title for the events on this timeline?**

1 The United States Becomes a New, Independent Nation

2 Slavery Comes to End in the United States

3 The Northwest Ordinance Is Passed

4 The United States Emerges as an Important Military Power

14 **The relationship between the national and state governments in our system of government is best described as**

1 democracy	**3** federalism
2 popular sovereignty	**4** checks and balances

15 **The main responsibility of the executive branch of government is to**

1 interpret laws	**3** carry out laws
2 make laws	**4** defeat laws

16 **In an outline, one of these is the main topic and the other three are sub-topics. Which is the main topic?**

1 Creation of the Cabinet	**3** Whiskey Rebellion
2 Washington's Administration	**4** Hamilton's Financial Plan

17

> "The great rule of conduct for us, in regard to foreign nations, is to extend our commercial ties and to have as little political connection as possible."
> — *President George Washington's Farewell Address*

Which opinion best reflects Washington's advice?

1   Americans must build a large and powerful army.

2   Americans should establish a global empire.

3   Americans should join military alliances to preserve their security.

4   Americans should avoid involvement in European alliances.

18 Under the "spoils system," President Andrew Jackson sought to

1   replace existing officeholders with members of his own party

2   stop one branch of government from becoming too powerful

3   limit the term of office of the Presidency

4   extend the charter for the national bank

19 Which developments were most important to the settlement of the West?

1   issuance of the Proclamation of 1763 and the Battle of Saratoga

2   completion of the Erie Canal and of the transcontinental railroad

3   the Dred Scott decision and passage of the Homestead Act

4   passage of Jim Crow laws and the *Plessy v. Ferguson* decision

20 The Monroe Doctrine involved the United States in the affairs of

1	Africa	3	Canada
2	Latin America	4	Asia

21 The term "manifest destiny" is most closely associated with

1	westward expansion	3	freedom of the seas
2	the Great Depression	4	World War II

22 During the Civil War, President Lincoln's primary goal was to

1	protect Southern slaves	3	preserve the Union
2	promote foreign trade	4	uphold the Confederacy

23 Which term best describes the type of economic system currently found in the United States?

1	mercantilism	3	communism
2	socialism	4	capitalism

Base your answer to question 24 on the poster to the right.

24 The main purpose of this poster was to
1   encourage westward migration
2   discourage future immigration
3   give land away to former slaves
4   increase urbanization

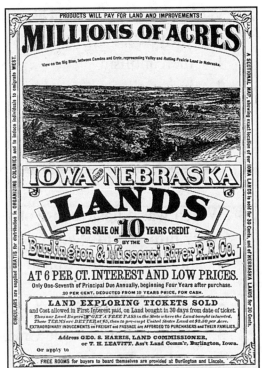

25 What was the main goal of the Women's Suffrage Movement in the late 19th and early 20th centuries?
1   obtain the right of women to join unions
2   gain the right to vote for women
3   expand the number of women managers
4   increase the pay of women workers

26 Workers organize into labor unions primarily to
1   improve their pay and working conditions
2   obtain ownership of the means of production
3   end racial segregation in factories
4   increase their production

27 Which was a major result of the Spanish-American War?
1   The United States emerged with a colonial empire.
2   The power of the federal government decreased.
3   Cuba became a new state in the United States.
4   United States expansion overseas came to an end.

28 The annexation of Hawaii, the Philippines and Samoa demonstrated the interest of the United States in
1   Central and South America
2   Europe and Africa
3   Asia and the Pacific
4   the Middle East

Base your answer to question 29 on the poster to the right.

29 **Which idea is best expressed by this poster?**

1   mercantilism
2   imperialism
3   patriotism
4   nativism

National Archives

30 **Which was a basic cause of United States entry into World War I?**

1   the desire of the United States to obtain colonies
2   defense of freedom of the seas
3   tensions between the United States and the Soviet Union
4   the German invasion of Poland

31 **Which event occurred immediately after World War I?**

1   creation of the League of Nations
2   agreement to create the United Nations
3   issuance of the Monroe Doctrine
4   purchase of the Louisiana Territory

32 **United States participation in World War I resulted directly in**

1   a stable international peace for the remainder of the century
2   religious conflicts within the United States
3   racial and religious harmony in Europe
4   a return to American isolationism after the war

33 **The "Harlem Renaissance" refers to the**

1   artistic style of the first settlers in New York
2   African-American soldiers in World War I
3   African-American literary and artistic achievements of the 1920s
4   rebirth of Hispanic culture in New York during the 1920s

34 Which invention brought the greatest change to American life-styles in the 1920s?

1   the railroad
2   the automobile

3   the steam engine
4   the computer

35 The most accurate statement about U.S. foreign policy is that it has

1   been guided by the national self-interest
2   consistently supported imperialism abroad
3   predominantly followed an isolationist policy since 1940
4   resorted to military force to solve all disputes

36 Which situation is most likely to occur in an economic depression?

1   New jobs are created by private businesses.
2   The government raises taxes to all-time highs.
3   There is a sharp decrease in available jobs.
4   A large number of new companies open for business.

37 Franklin D. Roosevelt's New Deal was an attempt to deal with

1   problems arising from World War II
2   hostilities between the Soviet Union and the United States
3   problems resulting from the Great Depression
4   discrimination during Reconstruction

38 The New Deal established the idea that

1   Presidents have little power to correct social problems
2   the government should own most industries
3   the government is responsible for overseeing the nation's economy
4   imperialism is the best way to guarantee markets for production

39 The purpose of the Nuremberg Trials was to

1   punish Nazi leaders for atrocities
2   stop the spread of communism
3   end fighting in the Balkans
4   resolve territorial disputes between Germany and France

40 One major cause of the Cold War was

   1   trade competition between the United States and Europe

   2   different political systems in the U.S. and the Soviet Union

   3   the rejection of Soviet membership in the United Nations

   4   the forced relocation of Japanese-Americans in detention camps

41

> "Separate educational facilities are inherently unequal. Therefore, … by reason of the segregation, the plaintiffs are deprived of the equal protection of the laws guaranteed by the Fourteenth Amendment."

What action was a direct result of this U.S. Supreme Court decision?

   1   Women were given the right to attend schools.

   2   World War II veterans were given educational benefits.

   3   Racially segregated public schools became illegal.

   4   Prison inmates were given access to educational programs.

42 With which statement would a follower of Dr. Martin Luther King, Jr. most likely agree?

   1   A law must be obeyed even if you disagree with it.

   2   Peaceful demonstrations against unjust laws are morally correct.

   3   Civil disobedience can never be justified.

   4   The use of violence is acceptable if the cause is just.

43 United States actions in the Vietnam War demonstrated that

   1   Communism was a superior system

   2   the United States has never lost a war

   3   advanced technology guarantees victory

   4   advanced weaponry cannot guarantee victory in all wars

44 The War Powers Act of 1973 sought to limit the power of the

   1   President   **3** Congress

   2   Supreme Court   **4** states

45 During the administration of President Bush, which important U.S. foreign policy goal was achieved?

   1   victory in the Korean War   **3** creation of a democratic Iraq

   2   the end of the Cold War   **4** American hostages in Iran were freed

PART II: CONSTRUCTED RESPONSE ITEMS

Directions (1–14): For each question, write your answer in the space provided. Use either pencil or pen to write your answers. If you want to change your answer, cross out or erase your original response. You may not know the answers to some questions, but do the best you can on each one.

I. *Base your answers to questions 1 through 4 on the cartoon below and your knowledge of social studies.*

The following cartoon appeared in various newspapers in 1901.

Library of Congress

1. What is the source of this political cartoon? _____ **[1]**

2. Which nation does the large, tall chicken represent? _____ **[1]**

3. Name two countries represented by the small chickens. _____

_____ **[2]**

4. State **one** provision of the Monroe Doctrine. _____

_____ **[2]**

II. *Base your answers to questions 5 through 8 on the map below and your knowledge of social studies.*

MAJOR CIVIL WAR BATTLES

5. What group is represented by the shaded area on the map? _____ [1]

6. According to the map, how many states were in the Confederacy? _____ [1]

7. What occurred at Vicksburg, Chattanooga, and Chickamauga on the map?

_____ [1]

8. Based on the map, why was the impact of the war more destructive on the South

than on the North? _____

_____ [2]

III. *Base your answers to questions 9 through 11 on the pie chart below and your knowledge of social studies.*

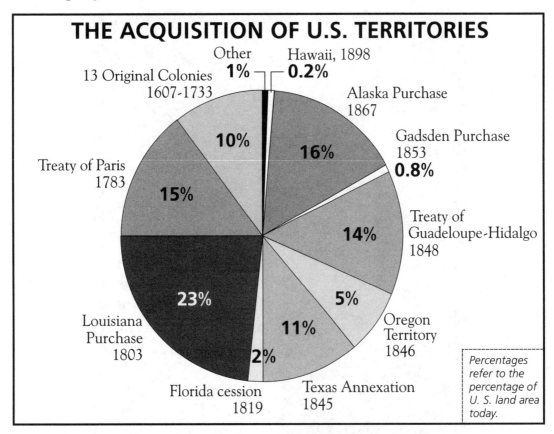

THE ACQUISITION OF U.S. TERRITORIES

Other **1%**

Hawaii, 1898 **0.2%**

13 Original Colonies 1607-1733

Alaska Purchase 1867 **16%**

Gadsden Purchase 1853 **0.8%**

Treaty of Paris 1783 **15%**

10%

Treaty of Guadeloupe-Hidalgo 1848 **14%**

Louisiana Purchase 1803 **23%**

5%

Oregon Territory 1846

2%

11%

Florida cession 1819

Texas Annexation 1845

Percentages refer to the percentage of U. S. land area today.

9. In what year did the United States acquire the Oregon Territory?

_____ **[1]**

10. In which century did the United States acquire most of its territory?

_____ **[1]**

11. State **one** major impact of the Louisiana Purchase on the growth of the United States. _____

_____ **[2]**

IV. *Base your answers to questions 12 through 14 on the poster below and your knowledge of social studies.*

Source: *National Archives*

12. What is the source of this poster? _____ [1]

13. What is the message of this poster? _____

_____ [2]

14. State **one** major objection the group responsible for producing this poster had to saloons in America. _____

_____

_____ [2]

PART III: DOCUMENT-BASED QUESTION

This question is based on the accompanying documents (1-8). The question is designed to test your ability to work with historical documents. Some of the documents have been edited for the purpose of the question. As you analyze the documents, take into account the source of each document and any point of view that may be presented in the document.

Historical Context:

Certain events in history are called "turning points" because of the significant impact they have on the direction that history takes.

Task:

Using information from the documents and your knowledge of social studies, write an essay in which you

Select **two** turning points from American history related to the documents, and for *each* turning point selected:

- *Describe* the event.
- *Discuss* why the event is considered to be a "turning point" in history.

PART A: SHORT ANSWER

Directions: Analyze the documents and answer the short-answer questions that follow each document in the space provided.

DOCUMENT 1

1. Based on the map, why was the failure of the British to succeed in this plan a major "turning point" of the American Revolution? _____

_____

_____

_____ [2]

THE BRITISH PLAN FOR TAKING NEW YORK, 1777

DOCUMENT 2

Construction Begun: 1819

Opened: 1825

Cost: $7,000,000

Length: 363 miles

Width: 40 feet

Depth: 4 feet

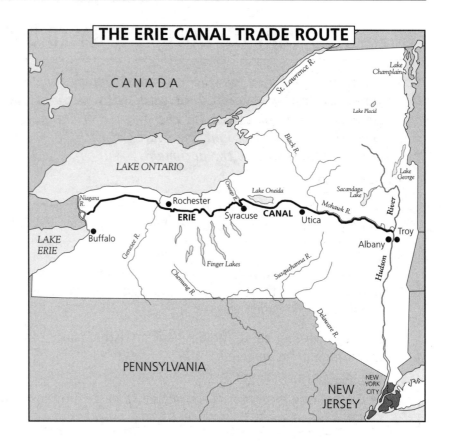

THE ERIE CANAL TRADE ROUTE

2. How did building of the Erie Canal make it easier to ship goods from New York City to the Western part of the United States? _____

_____

DOCUMENT 3

POPULATION OF CITIES BORDERING THE ERIE CANAL

Date	Albany	Troy	Utica	Syracuse	Rochester	Buffalo
1820	12,636	5,264	2,972	1,814	1,502	2,095
1825	15,971	7,859	5,040	3,833	5,273	5,141
1830	24,909	11,556	8,323	6,929	9,207	8,668
1840	33,721	19,334	12,782	11,013	20,191	18,213
1850	50,763	28,785	17,565	22,271	36,403	42,261

3. How was the opening of the Erie Canal a "turning point" for the cities along the route of the canal? _____

_____ **[1]**

DOCUMENT 4

SHIPPING FREIGHT: NEW YORK CITY TO BUFFALO

Route	Dirt Road (freight)	Canal (freight)
Method of Travel	Wagon	Boat
Amount of Time	20 days	8 days
Cost	$100 per ton	$15 per ton

4. According to the table, what effect did construction of the canal have on the cost of shipping freight from New York to Buffalo? _____

_____ [1]

DOCUMENT 5

5a. What is the "great event" that is described in this advertisement? _____

_____

_____ [1]

5a. How was this event a "turning point" in American history? _____

_____

_____ [2]

DOCUMENT 6

"The western country is rapidly filling up. A steady stream of immigrants is following the railroad lines and then spreading to the right and left. The vacant places still existing are either worthless or will soon be exposed to the same invasion. The plains are being occupied by cattle raisers, the fertile valleys and lowlands by [farmers], the mountains by miners. What is to become of the Indians?"

— *Carl Schurz, Present Aspects of the Indian Problem, 1881*

6. How was the building of railroads a "turning point" for the development of the

Far West? _____

_____ [2]

DOCUMENT 7

The U.S.S. Arizona burns and sinks at Pearl Harbor, December 7, 1941

7. What major event in U.S. history is taking place in this photograph? _____

_____ [1]

DOCUMENT 8

The New York Times

| VOL. XCI, No. 30,635 | TUESDAY, DECEMBER 9, 1941 | 3 Cents |

U.S. DECLARES WAR ON JAPAN

Over 1,500 Dead At Pearl Harbor
Aid Being Rushed to Hawaii

---

8. In what way did the event announced in this headline prove to be a "turning point"

in history? _____ **[1]**

PART B: ESSAY

Directions: Write a well-organized essay that includes an introduction, several paragraphs, and a conclusion. Use evidence from at least **four** of the documents in the body of your essay. Support your response with relevant facts, examples, and details. Include additional outside information.

Historical Context:

Certain events in history are called "turning points" because of the significant impact they have on the direction that history takes.

Task:

Using information from the documents and your knowledge of social studies, write the an essay in which you

Select **two** turning points from U.S. history related to the documents, and for *each* one selected:

- *Describe* the event.
- *Discuss* why the event is considered to be a "turning point" in history.

INDEX